A Necessary Joy

Yoga and the Quest for Transformation

Mark Gardett

Tehom Center Publishing is a 501(c)3 nonprofit publishing feminist and queer authors, with a commitment to elevate BIPOC writers. Its face and voice is Rev. Dr. Angela Yarber.

Paperback ISBN: 978-1-966655-56-5

Ebook ISBN: 978-1-966655-57-2

Contents

To all my trans siblings,
and to anyone who is struggling toward freedom.

"Once you are Real you can't become unreal again.
It lasts for always."

— *The Velveteen Rabbit*

Prologue

1.1 Now begins the practice of yoga.

THE FIRST WORD IN THE *YOGA SUTRAS* IS "ATHA": *NOW*. *ATHA* captures the very essence of liberation, which is to always be able to begin again, to be always at the beginning. In each moment, we can choose to realize our true Self, to react or not react to what is happening in our lives, to take one step on our chosen path or one step away. We aren't beholden to who we used to be, even one moment ago. In every moment, right now, we can become new or choose to stay the same. That choice is always ours.

It is always now. We are always beginning to practice. We begin now, and again now. In one minute, tomorrow, next year: we will always be beginning to practice. This is the very first *sutra*, the starting point and the restarting point.

Some versions of the *Sutras* say, *now begins the teaching of yoga,* or the exposition, or the understanding of yoga. Each of these, including the study of the original texts, are practices. One thing that all the translations agree on: yoga is not (only) an intellectual understanding. The heart, the core, the meaning of yoga is in practice.

Therefore I say, *now begins the practice of yoga.*

People grappling with their gender often ask, "I'm 25, am I too old to transition?" "I'm 40 . . . 50 . . . 70—is it too late?" No matter what you mean by transition, no matter whether you are trans or not, the answer is always no. It's not too late to begin now, nor is it too early, because now is the only available time.

So let us *now* begin this journey together without fear, because we can always come back and begin again.

Introduction

My first experience with yoga was in 2001. I had just graduated from college, and I was still living in Charleston, South Carolina, where I'd attended school. I think I must have had some concept of what yoga was from philosophy and world history classes in college, or interactions with the "hippie" culture that was thriving in Charleston at the time. But big box yoga stores hadn't started getting popular yet, and gyms were more focused on boot camps and high-intensity aerobics.

In other words, yoga wasn't big business yet. There were no yoga influencers, unless you count the gurus who came from India in the 1950s and 1960s to teach Westerners about the practice. Yoga was on the cusp of a visibility explosion, but it wasn't there yet.

That afternoon, I was heading into Earth Fare, the local organic grocery store (later to become a Whole Foods, of course), when I glanced over and saw a new storefront in the neat one-story shopping center on the other side of the parking lot. It was called Holy Cow Yoga. The sign featured a black-and-white cow sitting with crossed back legs, eyes serenely closed, with a small, inward smile on its face.

Whenever I see or encounter something that is going to become important in my life, I get a very particular feeling. Call it spidey sense or intuition or the backward repercussions of time in a quantum universe. Whatever you call it, I felt it powerfully that day. I could barely see the sign from where I was standing, but it felt significant in a way that could not be ignored.

Through my 25 years of practice, teacher training, scholarship, and sometimes conflict with yoga, that feeling has never gone away, only deepened. There is something about the practice of yoga that speaks to me and forces itself to be reckoned with. It is a powerful practice, and I felt that power, somehow, from across a parking lot on the way to buy groceries.

I looked it up just now. Holy Cow is still there. How lovely. From the photos, it looks exactly the same: the small, enthralling bookshop in the front with the texts that seemed to contain all the answers to my nebulous but pressing questions, and the neat, calm, wood-floored studio space where my anxiety melted away, if only for moments at a time.

I crossed to the storefront on that afternoon, not sure whether to go inside. In the front window, I saw a flier for a six-week introduction to yoga series.

That was it. A mundane errand, a glance out of the corner of my eye, the pull of something meaningful or important without knowing what it was or why, and then a phone call to my mother, asking her to get me the six-week class for my upcoming 21st birthday. She got me my first yoga mat, too, a pool-blue rubber-smelling rectangle that became a portal into another life. I still have it, although I've used many others, and eventually came to practice off my mat as well.

Yoga exerts this pull on many of us, for some reasons that touch the highest purposes of the human spirit and others that expose questionable motivations. It can seem exotic (*orientalized, colonized*), or like we can use it to get a kind of spirituality-light without the heavy lifting of religion. I'm highly aware of being a white person writing this book and undertaking this project.

The best I can say is that this is my own experience and my own practice. I have committed 25 years of my life to it and will commit the next 25 as well, in one form or another. I am sharing what I've learned in the hopes that it might shed some light on your path, not to provide authoritative answers.

Only a practice with some kind of human truth at its core can exert such a strong pull on so many people and generate so much debate, reinterpretation, and reimagination over so many centuries. Yoga, in some form, has existed for more than 3,000 years, and here we still are, sweating in Yoga Boxes and chanting in meditation centers thousands of miles and eons of cultural shifts away from its origins.

One of my teachers likes to start sentences with the phrase, "The yogis believe," but there is almost no way you could end that sentence that would be true. Yoga has spawned dozens or even hundreds of recognized texts and major traditions. The human truth at the core of yoga has driven continual reinterpretation, such that even Sri Swami Satchidananda, author of one of the most popular translations and commentaries of the *Yoga Sutras*, writes that "the truth of the Self is the same, but when presented to you through words and forms and modes, it may appear in different ways to suit the individual or the trend of the age."

"The truth can never be changed," he says. But the form, the practice, may change. Each guru, each practitioner, interprets the practice according to her life, her needs, her experience.

This book is the story of my life and my experience with the truths that I have found in yoga. Specifically, it is the story of my practice of yoga as a transgender person, from my earliest experiences with it, long before I even knew the word "transgender," through my darkest periods of self-hatred and depression, out into the open world of self-knowledge and transition, to my current practice, which of course is ongoing, neverending, always beginning again, and always, always as powerful as the deep, intuitive push that swerved me out of the other life I would have had and directed my feet to the door of the Holy Cow, to the sign advertising a six-week course, and to a practice without which I believe I would not still be here.

Why Is This Book Needed?

Transgender people stand right now at the center of a debate in our culture about the meaning of freedom itself. How much right do we have to follow our own path? To be self-determining and to seek an individual understanding of our true Self? What practices are we allowed to access in seeking alignment with ourselves?

These are also questions that lie at the heart of yoga.

Transgender, or trans, is a broad umbrella term that includes nonbinary, genderqueer, gender fluid, agender, and a lot of other people who may or may not always see themselves as aligned or part of the same community. What we all have in common is that we do not see our true selves in the gender that was assigned to us at birth.

Yoga is another broad umbrella term (perhaps even broader than trans), encompassing practices, beliefs, stories, experiences, and traditions that range from 3,000 years old to just invented yesterday, although not all yoga practitioners see all of these practices and beliefs as part of the same tradition. What all of these yoga traditions have in common is a particular goal. It's been phrased in many ways, but Sri Satchidananda puts it succinctly when he says that "our goal is to keep the serenity of our minds."

What, exactly, that means, or rather my particular way of understanding what it means, is the subject of this book. There are many terrific books out there about how yoga is good for your health or promotes wellbeing. That's not what this book is about. This book is about liberation.

Like trans people, many yoga practitioners arrived at yoga because they did not feel comfortable with what they saw or felt happening in the world. The constant seeking after pleasure, the productivity obsession, and the capitalist mindset of the world around them did not match their experience of, or longing for, a deeper Self. Whatever else they may argue about, all those who seek the liberation of yoga share a desire to know the deeper Self that lies below the turbulence of the world.

In other words, both yogis and trans people find themselves, at some point in their lives, pulled aside out of the rush and bustle and forward motion of their lives and stilled in front of a feeling they must acknowledge: the feeling that there is something *else*, something deeper and truer to themselves, down another path.

Yoga has been a light in the darkness for marginalized people since ragged bands of forest yogis began practicing strange austerities outside the city centers of Vedic life. The Vedic religion, the tradition just preceding yoga and in some ways informing it, was built around sacrifices to the Gods. That tradition belonged to the princes and the educated, who held the keys to all higher spiritual life and practice.

Yoga, as it is outlined in the Sutras and other early texts, may be so difficult that it could take you a thousand lifetimes to fully realize, but its lessons are accessible to anyone who is willing to try. As with transness, although there is a wonderful and growing community of yoga practitioners, yoga practice itself is solitary and individual. No one can do the practice for you, just as no one else can tell you your own experience of gender, how much (or little, or not at all) you want to "transition," or how your experience of gender will inform your life and choices.

Both of these paths are liberating, lonely, challenging, and strewn with obstacles, but at the end of each, there is the chance for a unique kind of abiding, settled joy in one's self and the world.

This book is needed now, in other words, because the complexities and challenges of the world are overwhelming us to the point of nearly unending conflict. Because trans people have become scapegoats when we could be beacons toward a new path of liberation, self-determination, and, yes, achieving the serenity of our own minds. Because we could be teaching one another how to follow our own paths to our Selves, rather than fighting over who deserves to use the bathroom.

Transness can help us understand the *Sutras* and how they can be applied in a complex, contemporary life, and yoga can help anyone going through a transformation by providing a blueprint for how to find and claim ourselves beneath the inevitable difficulty of change.

Transness as a Spiritual Practice

My story is the only one I can tell, and I believe that we learn more from each others' lives than from any tradition or text, no matter how powerful. I will offer my story as a set of stepping stones that you'll follow as you read the book, rather than all at once here in the beginning.

That said, I will tell you this:

I knew that I was *something* when I was four or five years old. I say *something* because I had no words for it. Certainly "transgender" wasn't a concept I was aware of. What I was very aware of was that the *something* should never, ever be talked about.

I believed that I would wake up one day with a "boy part." This wasn't a fantasy or a what-if, or even something I particularly wanted (because I knew that my parents, the people at church, and everyone else around me would see it as wrong and probably sinful). It just felt inevitable.

In fact, I hate telling this story because it's so difficult to express the feeling that something just is so, without even being conscious of thinking, "This is so." Mostly, I was surprised that other people didn't see it. It felt so *obvious*. That was part of what made it frightening, the sense that it could never be fully hidden.

As I say, you will hear more of my story throughout the course of the book. What I want to tell you here is that *being transgender*, whether that's nonbinary or agender or "binary" trans (moving from one end of the gender spectrum right over to the other, as in a trans man who shifts from being identified as female to identifying as male), *is innate.* Who knows why? You can think of it as a mismatched brain map if you want, at least for me. Inside was the brain map for whatever I am, something boy-ish near the middle of the gender spectrum called nonbinary/transmasc, and outside was this female body that just did not match.

Transgender, then, is a term to describe a person who experiences a gender mismatch.

Transness, as I'll define it, is something else. Something bigger. It's an experience all transgender people have, but it's not confined to transgender people. If it were more widely understood, I believe it could offer new insights and ways of being for *all* people.

That's the sense in which I say that transness is a spiritual practice.

When I came out as trans, first to myself, then to my close circle, and later to the world, I was faced with all kinds of questions and choices. Would I change my name? My pronouns? My body? Would my voice change? My face? My smell? The way my body built and rebuilt itself? The way it moved? The way people saw me and responded to me in the world? Would I be welcomed in some spaces and communities for the first time, and would I lose my membership in others?

Transness was the process of confronting these questions and then letting go, one piece at a time, of almost everything that human beings think of as the "self." My name. The body I had lived in my whole life. The way people saw me and identified me. The security of fitting into cultural, familial, and professional expectations.

My voice changed. I wore different clothes. Every aspect of how a person typically defines their self slowly dropped away.

And yet, I did not disappear.

The most profound lesson of transness is exactly this: beneath everything you think defines you is a true, abiding, and unchanging Self. I had been practicing yoga for nearly 20 years when I came out as trans, so I understood this idea at an intellectual level. It wasn't until I began to transition that I felt it and believed it.

Every time I let something go, I experienced all the emotions the *Sutras* talk about. I felt fear. I worried that I would make a mistake. I told myself stories I had learned from my family and my culture about what would happen and what kind of person I was becoming. And yes, I lost a lot. I lost almost more than I could stand.

But here is the difficult and liberating and complicated truth: I could stand it.

More than that, I *had* to stand it because as hard and full of grief as the losses were, it was worse to continue to live so far from what I knew to be my true Self. I had to get to a point where I literally could not live with the disconnect before I made the hard choices and changes that were required. I truly hope our culture gets to a point where no one has to feel that way before they can choose to live as themselves.

Transness as a practice, rather than a characteristic of an individual, is the conscious choice to let go of what we've told ourselves defines who we are, in order to find, underneath it, the deep and abiding Self—often in response to a realization that we are so far from the path of our true Selves that we must change or, if not die, then kill something vital in ourselves to keep living.

For those who know anything about the practice of yoga, this should sound familiar. It's not just a transgender experience. It is a profoundly, deeply human experience. It's why yoga continues to call to so many of us, around the world and from every walk of life, so many centuries after its beginnings in India. Yoga and transness are parallel practices toward the same goal of transformation.

Therefore I offer you my story, humbly and with profound respect for the difficult and complicated journey you are on simply by virtue of being human and for the many traditions on which I am drawing. It is the story of how transness finally taught me to understand the *Sutras* and yoga's guiding path to the Self, two decades after I first entered the door of a yoga studio and began to practice.

Welcome, and may you find a piece of your own puzzle in these pages.

The *Yoga Sutras*

The *Yoga Sutras* are a collection of very brief statements or instructions, each no more than a few sentences long. The word *sutra* is most often translated as "thread," as in the English word *suture*. The *Sutras'* brief, aphoristic instructions are the threads that, together, make up a particular form of yoga practice.

Much like Shakespeare, there are people who wonder whether Patanjali, the author of the *Sutras*, was one person. Generally, it's believed that he was. But it's also known that he didn't make up all the instructions he conveyed in his text. He brought together ideas from many previous oral traditions and texts, especially those known as the *Upanishads*. I'm not going to dive into the history and origins of the *Sutras* in depth here, but there are dozens of excellent, approachable books on the subject. Some of them are listed at the back of this book, in case you want to know more.

I chose to use the *Sutras* as the basis for my own exploration of yoga for a few reasons. In the first place, they are the most common basis for yoga teacher training programs and workshops in the United States, and they form the philosophical understanding, if any, that most Western yoga studio teachers bring to their classes and students. Since most of us as Westerners first encounter (and often only encounter) yoga in studio classes, the *Sutras* make up the yoga philosophy most likely to reach our ears—in one form or another, generally translated and re-translated and interpreted and re-interpreted.

Which is fine. Yoga is a system of thought and practice that has been re-interpreted by every generation and every culture that has picked it up.

I appreciated what I heard from my teachers, but I also found myself, about ten years into my own practice, wanting to understand more about what I was doing in these yoga classes. What was the purpose of the movements and breath patterns and words I was repeating? Yoga was becoming a deeper and more important part of my life with every year, and I didn't want to bring something so deeply into my life and heart and mind when I didn't know where it came from, or what it really meant.

The *Sutras* became my entry into the world of yoga philosophy. I have studied many versions, from traditional "direct" translations (with direct in quotation marks because translation is slippery and complex no matter who is doing it) to expansive modern interpretations, including feminist interpretations and commentaries that go far afield from the original text. I've listened, many times over, to readings of the text in the original Sanskrit— enough to memorize some pieces, although I do not speak Sanskrit.

You don't need to have read the *Sutras* to understand and

(hopefully!) benefit from this book. Although I have drawn largely from direct and often traditional translations, I'm not undertaking a sutra-by-sutra commentary. Anything you need to know from the texts, I will explain.

But I also don't want to make sweeping generalizations about yoga from no specific text at all. If we're going to grapple with what yoga can mean for modern Western people, I believe we must grapple with the tradition as it has been handed to us, even if we come to see it and live it differently than earlier practitioners did. I have infinite love and respect and gratitude for all those who have made the tradition of yoga available to us here. When I wrestle with how their ideas fit my 21st century transgender life, I truly believe I am undertaking the work they intended. Self-study is, after all, one of the key practices outlined in the *Sutras*.

There is far more in the *Sutras* than I have attempted to address. There is probably more in the *Sutras* than can be understood in a lifetime. My purpose is to grapple with a few concepts that lie at the heart of Patanjali's philosophy—especially those that I have struggled hardest to understand and integrate. I invite you with all my heart to seek out more information for yourself if the lessons here spark something in you.

The last thing I'll say about the text before we get to the juicy stuff is that Patanjali's method, or instructions, for yoga makes up just *one* thread in the much broader tapestry that is yoga. His is the yoga of "inner insight," or "the science of mental discipline," as Swami Satyananda Saraswati puts it. Other traditions include *bhakti* or devotional yoga (a more emotion-based form of yoga that relies on pure love of God, and which Patanjali refers to) and *karma* yoga (the yoga of action, suitable for those who practice through their work in the world), among others. There will be brief mentions of some of these other forms later in the book.

Patanjali's form of *raja*, or "royal," yoga is not the only path to the goal. There are as many paths as there are human beings. For many of us, however, the *Sutra's* lessons are among the most approachable. Patanjali lays out both the aim and the practices of yoga in a way that offers all of us insight into how to achieve the peace and self-knowledge that yoga promises. Very few philosophical or faith traditions offer such a comprehensive, practical how-to manual for achieving the aim of self-realization.

What the *Sutras* offer—or claim to offer—is a *way to live*, a guidebook for understanding why we suffer so much and how to be freer, happier, and more in touch with the truth at the heart of ourselves. That's not just for trans people, or "yogis." The lessons here are for everyone.

That's not to say, though, that they're easy lessons to learn.

The Struggle

I want to make it very clear that I'm not finished with any of the practices in this book. I'm mired deep in the common struggle of making sense of my life, doing the best I can, falling off my path and pushing through brambles and finding it again and being lured by shiny objects and all the rest of it. I'm not writing this as a guru, or as some kind of enlightened being. I like some things and dislike a bunch of other things. I have yet to achieve anything approaching equanimity regarding my noisy neighbors who throw parties on weeknights.

I'm offering this to you as one person's sincere effort to understand whatever lessons the *Sutras* can teach us about how to live. Like a lot of people, I wish I had a guidebook on how to make the "right" decisions in my life, and I keep hoping the *Sutras* might be it.

I've had a tumultuous relationship with Patanjali since the first time I picked up the text. I'm on my fourth copy of Satchidananda's version because I keep giving it away when I can't stand to even see it on my shelf anymore, then being compelled to buy another copy, only to read it, reject it, give it away, feel its absence, and start again. His was the first version I ever owned and read, and it's the most commonly used in training programs, so more than any other text, it has marked the ups and downs of my intimate and deeply ambivalent journey into yoga philosophy.

There have been times when I've literally thrown the book across the room or scrawled angry, gouging comments in the margins. The feminist and the social justice warrior are both strong in me. I own these terms without a qualm. I do not want to sit on the sidelines and observe with a calm smile on my face as the world tears itself apart. When the *Sutras* have appeared to me to dictate that course, I have stormed and raged against them, argued with them, torn my hair out over them. I've started and quit yoga training programs more than once because I couldn't find values I could align with.

Philosophy, meaning, self-knowledge, and finding my right place in the world are not trivial matters to me. They are the very food of my life, and as with food, what I take in becomes a part of my self. It is vitally important to me that what I ingest into my heart and soul and mind is not carrying disease with it.

If the *Sutras* can't offer us ways to live with complex, fundamentally human experiences like transness or changing technologies or cultural shifts, then they aren't what they say they are. They are meant to be instructions for living as a human, in the most deeply human possible way, connected to whatever is the true Self underneath everything that is *not*. If that promise is correct, the *Sutras* should give us, not esoteric theory, but a practical way of living in the world as it is.

The book you hold in your hands has not come easily. I have struggled and struggled with the meaning of these 196 brief, often opaque threads of text. The *Sutras* are not the be-all and end-all of meaning or even of yoga. They are not a religion; they don't say "do these things because they're right and God will bless you." Their teachings are closer to a question than an answer. They tell us: "Here is the cause of your suffering. What will you do about it?"

This book is my personal, hard-won, current (and likely far from final) answer to that question.

That's why this isn't a new "method" or brand or set of rules. I'm not proposing *transforming* as a kind of transgender Bikram. I hope that what you take with you is the permission, some of the tools, and a starting point to *transform the Sutras for yourself*. I do not believe that my life, or yours, has to be dictated in any way by what some guys wrote hundreds of years ago, but I do believe that if I'm going to study and practice yoga, I should do the work to come to terms with the tradition I'm asking to be part of.

It is that act of making sense of the practice for yourself that is transformative. As Sri Satchidananda says, "Study is all right—but not for mere logic, quoting, or fighting. Actually, it is only when you 'quote' from your own experience that your words have weight." That's what I've tried to do in this book. It is both my justification for writing it and my heartfelt offering to you.

Over the course of my 25 years of practice, the *Sutras* have enthralled me, taught me, made me furiously angry, felt deeply personal and almost insultingly distant, and brought me back again and again to peel back a new layer, and another, and another. With the *Sutras*, I am indeed always beginning again. I hope you will find as much to relish and gnash your teeth at and love in them as I have.

How to Use This Book

The *Yoga Sutras* offer a **description of the nature of reality** and a method of **letting go of everything impermanent** so that we can discover **the joy of union with the eternal Self**. They also show us **what stands in the way** of reaching that goal.

So this book offers my answers to the following questions:

- What is yoga? (Chapter 1)
- How should we practice? (Chapter 2)
- What must we do to prepare ourselves for yoga? (Chapter 3)
- What is the nature of reality? (Chapter 4)
- How can we know it? (Chapter 5)
- What keeps us from knowing it? (Chapter 6)
- What happens when we don't know it, or don't recognize it? (Chapter 7)
- Why bother with all this work? What is the promise of the yogic path? (Chapter 8)

Many have read the *Sutras* as a path out of suffering by disconnecting from the world, but that has not been my belief, nor my experience. In yoga, as in my trans journey, I have found joy and a new way, not to escape the world, but to join it fully. Yoga and transness are both practices of transformation, and transformation is my hope for you, as well.

For practitioners of yoga and students of the *Sutras*, may this book give you new insights and new ways to apply Patanjali's eternal lessons to your life and your practice.

For those in the trans and queer communities, may you hear the call to embrace your gender journey as a spiritual practice and a source of joy and meaning.

And for everyone who does me the honor of reading my words, may you find something to take with you that lights and lightens your way.

Chapter 1
The Quest

OVER THE COURSE OF THE MANY YEARS I'VE BEEN practicing yoga, I've heard it defined many different ways. "Yoga is union." "Yoga means 'to yoke.'" "Yoga means being fully present in the moment." "Yoga means aligning mind, body, and spirit." Even, "If you're breathing, you're doing yoga."

Each of these definitions captures something about the practice and purpose of yoga, but none of them reaches far enough. What Patanjali offers in the *Yoga Sutras* is nothing less than a description of the ultimate aim of life itself: liberation.

I went to a rodeo once with my parents. After a few little kids tried out their calf-roping skills to warm up the crowd, the energy surged, and everyone turned toward a heavy, barred gate, behind which a massive bull was being restrained while a man, who seemed tiny by comparison but was probably over six feet tall, climbed onto its seething back.

Everything you need to know about bull riding is in the name, except the sheer thrashing violence of it. To give you a sense of scale, the time required for a ride to count is a mere eight seconds. A full 85% of riders never make it past six seconds, and the majority of rides, about 60%, last less than four. The world record is 98 seconds. Injuries are common, and deaths aren't unheard of. That's how close to impossible it is to hold yourself onto a 2000-pound bull that wants you off.

What seems most incomprehensible about bull riding to those outside the culture is that it's so easy *not* to ride a bull. Just don't get on one. Or get off it, run away, and never come back.

Yoga tells us that there are a lot of things in our lives that we're riding like a bull—clinging to for dear life—because we don't realize we can get off, step into the stands, and watch the bull thrash around instead. We can stop grasping onto the whiplash-inducing up-and-down ride of life and achieve peace.

Letting go of the thrashing bull of our thoughts, emotions, and attachments is a lot harder than letting go of a bucking bronco. Eventually the bronco will throw you off. In our lives, though, we cling so hard that 98 seconds is nothing. I've got bulls I'm riding from 40 years ago.

Patanjali's offer is to teach us how to let go of the bull. His definition of yoga is worded slightly differently by various translators, but the meaning is the same: the work of yoga is to still the "fluctuations" or "changing states" of the mind, to "block the patterns of consciousness," to bring about the "cessation of the turnings of thought."

But the key to understanding the *Yoga Sutras* is that yoga is both a practice and a goal, and the two are not exactly the same. In fact, yoga is a widely varied collection of practices, from a number of interrelated but not identical traditions, that all aim toward one common goal. If Patanjali is a teacher, the *Yoga Sutras* are his syllabus. Like any other syllabus, he starts by outlining the goal, what you will have learned by the end of the course. In the *Yoga Sutras*, that's the first chapter, which includes the first 51 *sutras*. Each *sutra* is a short statement, often no more than a sentence or two. Taken together, the 195 (or 196, depending on who you ask) *sutras* make up the entire syllabus. The promise is that, if we follow these lessons, we will reach the final goal of liberation.

It might take a lifetime, or in the traditional belief system that includes reincarnation, it might take several lifetimes, or a thousand. Everyone, says Patanjali, will get there in the end. But just like every student in a class learns at a different speed, no two journeys to liberation will look the same. Because Patanjali's course promises to lead us to the very end goal and purpose of human life, to liberation itself, it will take longer, and require more from us, than a class that promises to teach us how to do long division or learn chemistry. Fortunately, yoga is also a massively expansive tradition, meaning that many, many paths and practices have been discovered that all lead to the same goal. So no matter what kind of learner we are, we can find a practice that will take us where we're going.

Undertaking the long journey to liberation will not leave us as we are. Without question, no matter what practice or tradition or path we choose, we will be transformed in the process. I spent many years as a teacher, and I can tell you that, without exception, learning changes us. In every moment, both teacher and student are being shifted and realigned. That happened even in classes where I was teaching Shakespeare or the five paragraph essay. How much more must it apply in a lifelong, or lifetimes-long, course toward personal liberation? Like the great quests of history and literature, Patanjali's syllabus will take us through the darkest parts of ourselves, through challenges we did not think we could overcome, into company we did not expect, and out the other side to joy we did not know was possible. And as Gandalf said to Bilbo Baggins in that other famous quest, *The Hobbit*: when we come back, we will not be the same.

Before we sign up for this quest to transformation, then, let us understand what, exactly, we are aiming for.

One Destination

When I was a kid, I loved the book *Ferdinand*. Ferdinand is a bull who doesn't want to fight. He loves to sit in the pasture and smell the flowers. When Ferdinand is finally forced into the fighting ring, he sits down to smell a flower and doesn't engage with the matadors, no matter what flags they wave in front of him. But then, disaster strikes! Ferdinand is stung by a bee and becomes enraged, throwing his horns and his hooves at everything around him. The bullfighters are finally happy, and they fight Ferdiand with all their might.

He's so successful in the fight that he is sent out to a pasture, where he can smell the flowers.

Oof, I get teary just thinking about that story. It's such a perfect encapsulation of the lessons of yoga. We start out in early childhood totally at one with the world, but as we grow, our inter-actions with other people and with the frustrations and other bee stings of reality cause our inner raging bull to thrash and kick and get generally excited and reactive. The goal is to go back to our true state of union with nature, or the divine Self: to rediscover the pasture and live calmly and with quiet joy.

That end state, the aim, is called *samadhi*. *Samadhi* has been translated in many ways over the centuries, as peace, liberation from suffering, or enlightenment. The direct translation of Patan-jali's third *sutra*, where he first introduces *samadhi*, is that the seer (that's you) abides in "his own true nature."

The aim, in other words, is *self-realization*. At the end of Patanjali's course, we will have let go of everything we believe to be ourselves, lifted the veil of ignorance that keeps us tied to impermanent things that can't really make us happy, and come to abide, permanently, in our own true selves. It is a transformative goal, but it's not the kind of transformation where you become something else. The transformation occurs as you lift away one layer after another of "not-me" to reveal what was always underneath, the reality of your union with the eternal Self that was always inside you.

Not unlike the journey of a trans person, it turns out. While from the outside, a trans person might appear to change into someone else, the internal experience is quite the opposite. They have finally set down the masks and expectations that are not their true self and revealed what was always within. In both cases, achieving the goal of self-realization brings peace and an end to suffering.

All of the roles we play, all of the ways we present ourselves in the world, all the faces we present to each other, are like clay figurines. We are constantly shaping and reshaping these figurines to fit how we want to be seen and how we want to see ourselves. There are child figurines and adult ones, perhaps figurines of one gender and then another, figurines that represent careers, relationships, and stages of life. As we practice, we come to see that all the figurines are in fact made from the same ball of clay. The clay is the underlying, unshaped self.

And beyond that, if we continue to practice, we come to an even more powerful realization: we are not the clay at all, but the sculptor. We can watch the playing and movement of the figurines and feel compassion for their trials and tribulations. We can do our very best to care for them and reduce their suffering. We can take care of our clay and mold and shape it with more intentional, gentler hands. But in the end, we will lay the clay aside. Our minds and bodies will be left behind, but the sculptor, the eternal Self, will remain.

The aim of yoga is first to realize the underlying self behind the figurines by breaking our identification with them, then to find union with the eternal Self so that we can let go of what is impermanent and find peace. At that point, we can live in the world in all of our various forms and yet all the time, remain aware that we are not the forms but the sculptor. That is bliss. That is freedom. I will use many stories and analogies and metaphors to describe it, but the goal always remains the same.

To reach that goal requires two things from us: practice and nonattachment. In syllabus terms, practice includes all the assignments and activities we take on to reach the desired aim. Nonattachment is the mindset with which we take those actions. We'll get to nonattachment in Chapter Six, but first, let's dive into the action at the very heart of yoga: the practice.

Or more accurately, the practices.

Infinite Practices

What image does the term "yoga practice" bring to mind? Perhaps you picture spandex-clad bodies moving through strange poses in a wood-floored studio, or monks in robes seated in silent meditation on a mountaintop. There's a lot of debate about what counts as yoga, but in essence, the only way to tell whether something is really yoga or not is by the goal.

Yoga practice is anything we do to move consciously toward the goal of liberation. If an activity helps me let go of my identification with the impermanent so that I can see the eternal Self more clearly, that activity can be part of a practice of yoga. One of the things people often miss when they first read the *Sutras* is that Patanjali was an astute student of human nature. He and the other early sages understood that the same path will not work for everyone, so the yogic tradition recognizes that people have different personalities, are in different stages of life, and live in different circumstances and cultural contexts, and therefore will need and want different ways to enter into practice.

Once you get closer to the end goal, to *samadhi* and the complete calming of the bucking bronco, the practices are more limited because the work is more subtle. But as far as starting points, there are as many ways into yoga practice as there are human beings. Patanjali offers quite a comprehensive list just for starters:

The supreme state of *samadhi*, he says, could come through faith, vigor, memory, contemplation, and/or by discernment.

Or it can be attained by total devotion to *Isvara*, the manifestation of the eternal part of the universe that is unchanging and unaffected by impressions and desires.

Or, "the practice of concentration on a single subject," or "the use of one technique" could get you there. You could work on cultivating the right attitudes towards different kinds of people: "friendliness toward the happy, compassion for the unhappy, delight in the virtuous, and disregard toward the wicked."

Or, the goal could be achieved by "controlled exhalation or retention of the breath." Or "concentration on subtle sense perceptions." Or concentrating on the "supreme, ever-blissful Light within." Or concentrating on the mind of a great soul like a guru, or concentrating on an experience you had during a dream, or by "meditating on anything one chooses that is elevating."

The "or," by the way, is part of the text. It's not an interpretation. Notice the comprehensiveness of these lists. Chanting. Breathwork. Faith. Discernment. *Vigor?* Concentration on . . . well, *anything?*

One commentator even notes that Westerners could practice concentration on something they're familiar with, like a tall building, as long as it is strong and stable. Whatever you concentrate on, he says, you will gain its qualities, so choose something or someone in your own environment that has the qualities you wish to cultivate, and start there. "To get to the point of complete dedication," Sri Satchidananda says, "many different routes are available: hundreds of paths, religions and philosophies, all with one ultimate goal. It is immaterial what we do to achieve it as long as we achieve it."

Even your doubts and skepticism can be a starting point. That's where this book first began. When I first read the *Yoga Sutras*, I had some pretty serious reservations. Concepts like *karma* and *nonattachment* didn't sit well with me (we'll come back to them later in detail). I'd had too many experiences with people who tried to escape the world or abdicate their responsibilities, and I didn't want to take up a practice that advocated aloofness or escapism.

Those doubts led me to read the yogic scriptures. I read every translation I could find, from traditional interpretations to expansive and even radical ones. I studied not only Patanjali's scriptures, but texts from other yoga traditions, as well as Buddhism and other closely related systems. I read them all again.

As I read, I saw that, yes, the translations were different, and the ideas were stated in different ways, but there were also underlying patterns and similarities that pointed to the deeper truth beneath the variances in interpretation. I began to experiment with those deeper truths, taking up practices that appeared in multiple texts and watching their effects in my life.

My doubts, in other words, led me here. In Patanjali's terms, that makes sense because each person practices according to their own inner nature. I recently asked my brother and a few of my closest friends what words they would use to describe me, and "obsessed with finding the truth" and "always questioning everything" came up in every conversation. I'd love to think that I'm the kind of person who is laid back and easygoing, the kind of person who could settle comfortably into yoga practice and just enjoy the benefits. But I'm not. Coming to that understanding of myself so that I could know where to start was in fact the first part of my practice.

Start where you are, as you are. You can enter through the doors of a big-box yoga chain and find your way to *samadhi* in time. If you are a scholar, study. If you are a person of action, act, and then apply the questions raised by the *Sutras* to evaluate and shift your actions. If you are a person of faith and devotion, pour your heart into contemplation of a person you admire. Most of us are some combination of all of these things, and so our practice may include many parts. All the better.

To mix metaphors, whatever door you are standing at now is a door you can enter through. Perhaps when you enter, you will find the path that leads to yoga. Perhaps you will find another path, or another type of practice. According to Patanjali, we will all get there in the end. But if you want to enjoy the benefits, you have to start.

In a sense, *samadhi* is the Nobel Prize of yoga. Those of us who claim to be practicing yoga should have our eyes turned toward that final aim. But a high school chemistry student isn't expected to do Nobel Prize level work—-not even the future Nobel Prize winners. In yoga, we are all future Nobel Prize winners. We will all reach the aim. For now, though, we start with the practices we are ready for. Fortunately, the tradition is extremely generous. There are as many places to start as there are individuals in the world.

That said, most of these practices are handed down to us through specific traditions. Practicing within a specific tradition can simplify matters by providing a blueprint. It can also raise a lot of questions, especially for Westerners. How we understand and work within those traditions says as much about us as individuals as it does about the traditions themselves.

Many Traditions

When I was about ten, my family went to a production of *Fiddler on the Roof*, a musical about a strict Jewish family caught between the old ways of their culture and the fast-changing modern world. If you've ever seen the musical, you probably remember the turning point when Tevye, the father of the family, is contemplating allowing his daughter to marry a young man she loves instead of the much older man the traditional matchmaker has picked out for her.

He goes back and forth, arguing with himself. On the one hand, the children love each other, and on the other hand . . . *tradition!*

I saw the musical more than thirty years ago, but the utter conviction with which Tevye said that word still rings in my ears. It encapsulates everything he has ever known. Tradition has driven every choice in his own life. Now the people he loves are asking him to change. What is he losing if he gives it up?

But on the other hand, what is he losing if he grips it too tightly?

Those of us who choose to practice yoga, especially in the 21st century, especially in the West, especially people not of Indian descent, find ourselves wrestling with this question a lot. On one hand, yoga is a personal practice. Everything I said about practicing in a way that fits your personality and your stage of life is true. But on the other hand, what about the tradition? And for that matter, which one?

The sheer number of books written about the history of yoga, and the amount of argument about their accuracy, suggests how complex and intricately woven that history is. To start with, yogic psychology recognizes four basic kinds of people: emotional, intellectual, active, and contemplative or mystical. There is a tradition, or type of practice, appropriate to each of these types. Emotional people can follow *bhakti*, or devotional, yoga. For intellectual types, there's *jnana*, the study of scripture. Active people need a way to practice while being part of the world, and for them there is *karma* yoga, or the yoga of work. Patanjali's *Sutras* make up the primary text of the *raja yoga* school, the so-called "royal" yoga, for contemplatives.

There's also a recognition that most of us aren't purely one type or another, so our individual quest is likely to be a mix of practices. Moreover, yoga is also aware that people change over the course of their lives. A young student, a busy parent, and a retired person are likely to have different practices as well.

Then there's *hatha* yoga, which is the basis for most of the physical practices that we think of as yoga here in the West. Historical evidence suggests that *hatha* yoga has origins in ancient *tantric* Hinduism—and indeed Hinduism, Buddhism, and other religious traditions from the region have all influenced, been influenced by, and interwoven with yoga in various ways over the past 3,000 years. To make things even more complicated, many of the specific poses now practiced in yoga studios were introduced to India in the past two centuries via colonialism. Yoga is definitely what's known as a syncretic tradition, meaning that it's made up of a combination of different philosophies, beliefs, and faiths that are now so interwoven as to be difficult to fully separate.

For us as practitioners, that has benefits and drawbacks. The benefit is that there are so, so many paths available to reach the ultimate goal. Whoever you are, whatever type of person you are, whatever kind of practice is most aligned with your personality, you can find a yoga tradition, and a yoga practice, to lead you to liberation. That's why I say that the tradition is generous.

For those who prefer certainty that they are doing the "right" practice, however, the syncretism of the tradition is a major stumbling block. I've seen enough squabbling among practitioners about whose lineage is older, or more "traditional," or has been in unbroken operation longer, to know that yogis are not above a little sibling rivalry.

Ultimately, for better or worse, it's up to you to decide how much it matters to you to be part of a particular tradition or lineage. It's worth knowing, though, that every scripture I've read emphasizes that it is not possible to reach the ultimate goal through scripture alone. Eventually, you have to put the books down, undertake your own practice, and experience union and liberation for yourself. It's a long road, and like any learning path, following what teachers have already laid out for you is more important at the beginning, when you're just getting started. The further along you get, the more you'll have to practice and experience it for yourself.

Honoring the tradition you want to be part of is both respectful and, let's be honest, practical. Generations of intelligent human beings have dedicated their lives to developing the tradition as it stands: the practices, the concepts, the yogic way of understanding the world and the human mind. Why reinvent every one of these wheels from nothing? "There is this advantage in it," writes Sri Satchidananda; "instead of your trying this and that and wasting time, you ask a person who already knows the way." On the other hand, he says, "if you can select for yourself, go ahead."

It's also instructive to read what he says on the subject of *gurus* (teachers) and role models. "Many people do not have that much confidence in their own hearts." They are very aware of the "rubbish" (as he puts it) inside themselves and think that they cannot possibly be their own teachers. For these people, he recommends dwelling on "the heart of a noble person," someone who has the attributes they wish to attain. The idea of giving yourself over completely to a *guru* is derived more from a traditional understanding of yoga and other religious practices in India than from the *Sutras* themselves, and Edwin Bryant, among others, raises warnings about "charismatic" gurus and the danger they have caused throughout the history of yoga.

Study the history behind what you are doing. Understand the actual aims and purposes of the practices you choose to undertake. These are signs of respect and humility very appropriate to a beginner in any tradition. As you start to understand the various traditions and paths available, you may find yourself changing and moving around. Your practice may shift as you move through different stages of life. The more I study yoga, the more I find that the ancient authors understood human beings pretty well, both their ultimate potential and their foibles, distractions, and needs. Thus all the different options for practice.

But don't get sidetracked into nitpicking the meaning of this or that text, or arguing about whose lineage is most "pure." These are distractions from the ultimate goal that the sages themselves warn against. Wherever you are, undertake a practice wholeheartedly, study it intentionally, and let it guide you.

Transforming

It's always informative to see how someone reacts when I tell them I'm trans. Some reject me outright. Others are excited or welcoming. Still others just don't care. Sometimes, they act like I've just told them I have a disease, making a frowny face and offering their support.

I've learned that their reactions have far more to do with them than with me. And I will absolutely take allyship wherever I can find it, in any form. The political situation for trans people is scary. I am grateful to anyone who supports our right to exist, even though I think it shouldn't be a question for other people to decide.

Being trans has personal, political, and physical implications. It can make life more difficult in material ways. It's a matter of discussion and debate among people who don't know the first thing about it, or about me.

But from my perspective, none of that is the most important thing about being trans. The most important thing is that it's *fascinating*.

I spent my whole life wanting to be someone else. I didn't quite know why, but I knew that I didn't want to be me. I fantasized and wrote stories and imagined other lives constantly. I moved around and tried out different careers and clothes and hobbies. No matter what I did, there was still that feeling of something wrong, of wanting to be someone else. Then I discovered the word "transgender," and suddenly it made sense. That was the beginning, but it wasn't the interesting part. The interesting part was getting to watch myself change.

It's almost impossible to know just how different you could be from how you are now, and still be yourself. That's not sad or a problem to be dealt with. It's *amazing*.

Before I started transitioning, every question about the process raised fear and uncertainty. What would I look like? Sound like? Feel like? Underneath all of that was the real question: *Would I still be me?* Discovering that everything I thought of as myself could change without touching the fundamental being underneath was utterly liberating and, as I say, endlessly fascinating. On the outside, everything about me changed, but on the inside, I finally no longer wanted to be someone else.

Yoga presents the same kind of paradox. It asks you to lay aside everything you identify with, all the external markers of "you," and to change utterly—in order to see that, at a fundamental level, you cannot change. The eternal part of yourself was always there and will always be there. And that, also, is amazing.

In his commentary on the *Bhakti Sutras* (the *bhakti*, or devotional, equivalent of Patanjali's *Yoga Sutras*), Swami Prabhavananda tells the story of a holy man and a king: "The king came to the holy man and said, 'You are such a great soul, you have such great renunciation.' The holy man replied, 'Oh, no, you are the greater man of renunciation. You see, I have renounced the finite, puny, ephemeral things, for that which is infinite and everlasting. But you have renounced the eternals for the noneternals of life. Hence your renunciation is greater than mine.'"

Yoga is, according to Patanjali, the highest aim of life. To practice yoga is to seek after the ultimate truth and an unending connection with the eternal, divine Self. It is the opportunity to give up the impermanent, the unimportant, and the ultimately unfulfilling to pursue eternal bliss and freedom. Yes, there is a risk to being openly trans in this political climate. And yes, yoga might ask you to give up some of the behaviors, or parts of yourself, that have most defined you, or that you thought most defined you. But both transness and yoga are also adventures of the highest order.

They are parallel journeys on the adventure—the quest—of transformation. Nothing in my own life has ever been more exciting, more thrilling, or more worthwhile. The risk is rewarded ten thousand times. I've had people tell me that yoga seems boring or that gender doesn't matter, but these two practices of uncovering my true self have been the least boring and most meaningful things I've ever done.

As on any quest, I have run into monsters, both without and within. I have faced challenges and pain that I thought I would not survive. The path is not an easy one. You may find yourself in places that are bewilderingly different from where you thought you were headed. When the goal is as lofty as ultimate reunion with the true self, the road will be hard in equal measure. But throughout, if we keep our eye on that final goal, we will arrive.

Whatever tradition you choose, whatever scripture you follow, whatever practices you undertake, you will find success eventually if you commit to the quest. "This statement," Swami Saraswati says, "includes all paths and techniques of yoga. None are excluded. They all lead to success." The one requirement is dedication.

**I prepare myself for practice by asking,
"What scares me about the promise of
transformation?
What desires push me forward toward self-
knowledge? What do I hope to find or to become?"
I know that I can choose what quest to undertake,
and I remind myself that transformation is not a
path away from myself, but toward freedom.**

Chapter 2
Commitment

ONE OF THE MOST MOVING AND POWERFUL SPIRITUAL experiences I've ever had occurred when I was eight or nine years old. The week before Easter, I stayed up late, put on my church clothes in the middle of the night, and went with my mother to sit in the church and pray.

It was exciting just to be up late at night and to be doing something that seemed so grown up, and when we entered the darkened, nearly empty church, goosebumps ran up and down my entire body. I had never seen the church dark before, or felt the kind of absolute silence that fell over us as soon as the door closed. Candles were lit at the back and front of the long, red-carpeted aisle, and I could just see the dim shapes of a few bowed heads here and there among the long rows of pews.

My mother motioned me to silence, but I don't think I could have made a sound if I'd wanted to. The expectation of reverence was palpable.

As we walked up to the aisle to find a pew, I saw a large sign I'd never seen before. On it were the words, "Could you not watch with me one hour?" I still remember the chills and the sense of responsibility that rushed through me when I saw it. We were there in honor of Jesus's night in Gethsemane, where he was arrested and taken to be tried and then crucified. On that night, Jesus asked his disciples to wait and watch with him. He knew what was going to happen to him, and he wanted company in his prayers. Yet one by one, the disciples fell asleep, and Jesus was left alone with the terrible knowledge of what he was going to face.

My mother and I have had what could at best be called a tumultuous relationship. She has not spoken to me since I came out as trans. But we shared something—we share something—that suggested she should bring me with her, young as I was, to experience that night of prayer. I've spent many years trying to figure out what that shared something is. It's somewhere between mysticism and the capacity for absolute devotion. I know that at that moment, in that church, I wanted to lay myself at God's feet and cry out for his poor son. I wanted, more than anything, to believe I would have been able to watch for that one hour.

Fortunately for me, the capacity for devotion—the willingness to commit to a path or a practice with your whole heart and stick with it—is the primary requirement for the transformational quest that is yoga.

The Royal Road

The method that Patanjali lays out in the *Yoga Sutras* is *raja yoga*, the so-called "royal road" on the quest to *samadhi*. If *bhakti* yoga lays out a path of worship, or devotion to a personal representation of the divine, and *jnana* yoga lays out the path of scriptural study and rationality, *raja* yoga is the path of contemplation or self-study. Patanjali provides a series of what might be called psychic exercises that lead the student progressively deeper into the psyche, from the surface layer of behavior all the way down to awareness of the subtlest movements of the unconscious.

Which specific practices you choose to undertake will depend on your personality, your stage of life, and all the other variables we talked about before. But in order to move forward on our quest, whatever practice we choose must be undertaken as *abhyasa*. *Abhyasa* is sometimes translated simply as "practice," but it describes not so much a "what" as a "how."

Abhyasa has been called "effort toward steadiness of mind," "to be established in the endeavor," and "the effort to be fixed in concentrating the mind," among many others. What they all have in common is the focus on commitment, rather than any particular behavior. Practice becomes "firmly grounded," Satchidananda says, "when well attended to for a long time, without break and in all earnestness."

Earnestness. I love that. Others call it reverence. Devotion. *Zeal.* Lovely, lovely words for the commitment required to stay on our quest. A person who can twist themselves into the most impressive poses but is thinking about something else the whole time isn't doing yoga. On the other hand, to eat an apple in complete devotion to the experience of that apple, with reverence for the entire system of nature from which it came and earnestness in thinking only of that apple, could be a practice of yoga without doubt.

My favorite of the practice words is *zeal.* Devotion, earnestness, and reverence can all evoke the still silence of church or the concentrated hush of a professor's study. Zeal is closer to joy, enthusiasm, and passion. Zeal tells us that our practice shouldn't be dull or plodding, no matter how devoted. It can be play! Love of life! To practice with zeal is to practice with excitement, wonder, and a sense that absolutely anything might happen.

Part of my own practice is what I call "poeming." I go out into the world—to the park, or a nature trail, or a pond, or even just around my neighborhood here in the city—and stop regularly to look at small, individual parts of that world closely. I might bend down and examine a leaf or sit in a stand of trees or say hello to a dog, but whatever I do, I try to see the world with zeal for all its potential. I call it poeming because, for me, this is also the practice that leads to writing poems. But the poem is the byproduct. Poeming, the act of being closely, enthusiastically, devotedly aware of the world, even if only for a few moments, is the practice.

Not everyone will respond to poeming, and that's fine. Each person's practice not only will look different, but *must*. After all, passion and devotion and zeal are aroused in each of us through different means.

A Sweet Dish

Given that the practice of yoga could apparently look a lot of different ways, how do you decide where to start? My favorite answer to this comes from Swami Saraswati, who writes that whatever you choose to focus on in your practice, it "must be chosen to suit the inherent nature of the mind and personality." Whatever you choose must be so absorbing that you are *consumed* by it.

"There must," he says, "be spontaneous attraction."

In fact, he goes farther, in one of my favorite lines in any translation of any yoga text in history: the practitioner, he says, "should love his practice as he loves his body. He should be as attracted towards the practice as he is towards a sweet dish of his choice. The practices can produce the desired result only if they are done with love and attraction."

Sit with that for a moment. Love. Attraction. To be drawn to practice as to a "sweet dish" of your choice. To love and desire and yearn for your practice the way you yearn for ice cream on a hot day. How utterly different this picture is from the picture of self-denial that we so often associate with spiritual commitments.

Yoga recognizes at least four different types of people, very similar to the personality types that have been identified in cultures from Ancient Rome to Jung. There are people who are primarily active and practice through labor, those who are primarily contemplative and inward-looking, those who are emotional and drawn to devotion and worship, and those who study and learn through thoughts. Each and every one of these types can achieve the goal of yoga through their own, spontaneously attractive, aligned means. You can get there by reading texts or by wholehearted worship or by inward contemplation of the type that Patanjali focuses on.

What, then, makes a practice *yoga* and not just a thing you're already doing? From my study of the *Sutras*, I've come to believe that three things are needed:

First, the practice you choose must actively and intentionally work toward the final aim of liberation: stilling the mind and the body so that union with the eternal Self can be restored. The practice must be aimed at getting yourself off that bull and toward *samadhi*.

Second, it should be undertaken seriously, with devotion and *zeal*. That's why choosing a practice that fits you is so important. Otherwise, you won't be able to feel enthusiastic enough to persist in the long-term process of slow disentanglement that is the goal.

Finally, it cannot cause harm. The various commentaries offer different ways to think about this, but it's also pretty straightforward. And by the way, it includes harm to yourself.

You may never (okay, probably will never) achieve the Nobel Prize-level yogic experiences, but if you do, it will come naturally as part of whatever practice you devote yourself to. You cannot force yourself to be a yoga master or a guru or enlightened. The harder you force, the farther away you'll be. As someone with a lot of will power and an enormous amount of physical energy, this is one of the lessons of the *Sutras* that drives me bananas. I want to power through it! Alas, that's never going to be the answer.

What I can master, and what you can master, is our own practice, now, where we are, as we are, with commitment and earnestness. Discover what spontaneously attracts you toward the goal and devote yourself to it. Everything follows from that. When you find the right practice, you will be drawn to it as a sweet dish you cannot keep yourself away from.

One Vow

The sheer number and variety of practices available to the aspiring practitioner can be overwhelming. There's no way to start with all of them, and I know that, for myself at least, when I first started yoga, I probably didn't know myself well enough to consciously choose the "sweet dish" that would serve me best. That's why Sri Satchidananda suggests we make a single vow, practice one method, or "achieve one pose." "By practicing just one of these virtues," he writes, "all the rest will follow."

The most famous example of organizing an entire life around a single vow is Gandhi. In his quest to liberate not just himself but the entire country and people of India, Gandhi committed himself wholly to the principle of *ahimsa*, or nonviolence. No matter what was done to him, no matter how he was treated by the British powers that ran India at the time, he refused to respond with violence. He was beaten by police when he took a seat on the coach that was reserved for Europeans. He was jailed. And through it all, he remained steadfast in his commitment to nonviolence—and was successful where violent uprisings had failed.

Many leaders of the American Civil Rights movement followed his lead. Martin Luther King, Jr. advocated nonviolence, having seen its effectiveness and its power to bring people into the cause. Like Gandhi, Rosa Parks refused to move from her seat on the bus but also refused to respond to hatred with anger, or to violence with more violence.

In the Hindu pantheon of Gods and demigods, Hanuman, the monkey god who is the son of Vayu, Lord of the Winds, is the living representation of the virtue of *brahmacharya*. Sometimes translated as celibacy, *brahmacharya* literally means to follow Brahma, or to devote oneself to the divine without cease. Hanuman was so committed to Lord Rama (one of the incarnations of the God Vishnu) that, to demonstrate his devotion, he tore open his chest. Lord Rama and his consort Sita were seated there, where Hanuman's heart should have been.

We're not likely to become Gandhi or Hanuman or Martin Luther King, Jr., but we can follow their example in making one vow, one commitment, and following it wholeheartedly, with zeal and earnestness. And again, the vow we choose is likely to be one that fits our own personality and natural way of relating to the world. In fact, when you choose where you want to start, you're likely to find that you have already been aligned with one of the practices or methods of yoga without being aware of it.

My own vow, the primary focus in my quest, has been *svadhyaya*. *Svadhyaya* is often translated as "self-study," and it can include a variety of methods, from reciting the scripture (study of the Self through recorded tradition) to literally studying your own self, including your reactions to the world, your patterns of behavior, and your mental habits. These two sides of the *svadhyaya* coin in fact work together: the scripture provides a framework for understanding the behaviors and patterns you see in yourself, and increased self-awareness shows you how the lessons of the Scriptures play out in your own life. It's a recursive and ever-deepening practice of self-knowledge and understanding.

Svadhyaya fits my natural way of being. I was already studying myself long before I ever heard of yoga. Studying is something I do naturally. About a month into graduate school, one of the other students came up to me and said, "Word on the grapevine is that you're studious." I was stunned for a moment. *Aren't we all studious?* He was also there to earn a PhD. He also barely knew me. Anyone in the "grapevine" he was referring to couldn't have known me more than a week or two. But like it or not, we are who we are. Committing to a lifelong practice, to a quest, is not easy. Pursuing it in a way that makes use of our inherent nature puts it that much closer to our reach, especially at first.

Given that the end goal of yoga is reunion with the true, eternal Self that lies beneath the temporary forms of daily life, it makes sense that self-study could be an effective path. But any one of the many options will lead you to the same destination. Again, the key is not what you do, but how you do it. The most austere practice in the world, undertaken without *abhyasa* or devotion to the final aim, will never get you there. Making a single vow and keeping it, though—loving it as an increasingly important and meaningful part of your life, organizing yourself around it with the aim of transformation and reunion—cannot fail. It may take years or decades or lifetimes, but it will lead you where you need to go.

Transforming

A great deal has been said about transgender "regret," the idea that trans people who pursue medical or surgical or other physical transition will come to regret it once it's too late and the changes are permanent.

To these people, I say: welcome to life.

Deciding to undergo any form of physical gender transition is a lot like deciding to get a tattoo. You are making a change in your body that is (to a greater or lesser extent) permanent, and yes, you will have to live with it.

Before I got my first tattoo, I had the experience many people have. I bit my nails and changed my mind and went back and forth on design ideas and thought, "How can I possibly know what I'll want on my body *for the rest of my life?*" I finally made up my mind to go ahead with it and made an appointment with an artist. For the two weeks before the appointment, I was fearful and nervous. What if I hated it? What if it hurt too much? What if he messed it up? So many things could go wrong, and it would be *permanent!*

When I finally arrived at my appointment, it was completely different from what I expected. The studio was full of artists collaborating with clients, talking about size and color and meaning. One man was getting a collection of *Star Wars* themed pieces up the entirety of one leg. No one there questioned the idea of being so committed to something that you'd have it inked onto yourself.

I asked my artist about the potential for regret, and he said, "It's not a question of knowing you're still going to love it when you're 80 or whatever. I have pieces that aren't my favorite, that I might do differently now. But I love them because they remind me of that moment in my life, who I was then. The meaning of them changes over time. They're important to me in a different way now."

Gurus, my friends, are everywhere. This young man, with tattoos even on his *eyelids*, a person a lot of people would move away from if he sat next to them on the bus, offered me an insight that I've taken into every decision I've made since then.

Making a commitment, even an irreversible one, does not mean you will never change. It doesn't even mean you'll have no regrets. The only kind of life with no regrets is one where you make no decisions at all, and I'm afraid that's not possible. Even choosing not to make any choices is a choice. It's one of the paradoxes of being human. The people agonizing over "what I'll still want on my body in thirty years" and never deciding may well end up regretting that choice, too. Who knows?

If the first and most important step in yoga is simply to decide on a practice and commit to it, to love it like a sweet thing you can't resist, then yes, commitment will remove other choices. Living with that reality is what makes a commitment meaningful.

If we never had to give anything up, our choices would have no power.

I'm not saying that choosing not to have tattoos indicates a lack of ability to commit. If you know you don't want any, great. You're choosing to put your energy and your devotion into something else. The suffering comes not from choosing one thing or the other, but sitting in the middle of the seesaw, leaning back and forth, wringing your hands and wondering *what if?*

My experience with tattoos helped me make the decision to start taking testosterone, and later, the decision to get top surgery— and since then, the decision to reduce my testosterone slightly and to not pursue any other forms of physical transition. Tattoos taught me that the practice isn't in the choice of getting a tattoo or not getting one. In that moment, you simply make one choice or another. The practice is how you live with the choice you made. How it shapes you. How you respond to the way it shapes you, and the ways it shapes other people's perceptions of you.

I know many queer and trans people caught in the middle of the transition seesaw. Spending the time to understand what you really want is vital. But putting off a decision that you know to be right for yourself because someone might see you differently, or because you might lose something in gaining something else, is not relieving your suffering. The meaning of a choice cannot ever be understood until it's made. This is the challenge of commitment: to commit to one thing means to let go of others.

There's an idea that, to truly practice yoga, you have to become a vegan, give up coffee and sugar and everything else you enjoy, and sit still until you achieve the gold star of a blinding light in your mind that eliminates your desire for cupcakes.

I'm not making fun. I know this image well because it was my own.

Practice is something else altogether. Practice is the slow, life-changing process of making commitments and seeing how they change you. It's not even making commitments and then *sticking to them forever no matter what.* Your commitments may change, just as my tattoo artist's feelings about his earliest tattoos had changed.

I've never gotten a "flash" tattoo, where you walk into a studio, point to one of the pictures on the wall, and say, "I'll have that one." Every one of my pieces is an individual, thought-out, and unique piece of art. I love every one of them, and their meaning changes and deepens the longer I have them. But in every single tattoo shop I've ever gone into, I've heard some variation of the statement that, "You know, I think my flash pieces are some of my favorites." There's something to be said for walking in, making a choice, taking what's available, and then shaping your life, in some small or large way, around the new reality you've made.

How else do we know ourselves than through the decisions we make and the ways we learn to live with them? And for that matter, what choice do we have? Like you, I'm forced to live with the past. Many, many things happened to me over which I had no control. These experiences changed me in ways that I will never fully understand because there's no way to go back and compare myself with the other, alternate, "would have been" version.

The past is like a tattoo you got at 18 that you're now stuck living with. How you live with it defines you much more than the tattoo itself does.

When I decided to get top surgery, I knew that there was some chance that a later version of myself would disapprove. I knew there was much I could lose. I'd already lost deeply important people in my life just by coming out as trans. Getting top surgery, even more so than going on testosterone (which is largely reversible), was a declaration, a public commitment: this is who I am now. It forced other people to come to terms with parts of myself I had spent forty years hiding.

It forced me to come to terms with them, too.

I love all my tattoos, and I love, love, *love* my flat chest and the fact that when I happen to see myself in a reflection, I am still floored with gratitude to see a body I recognize as my own—a body I never thought I would be able to inhabit. This body feels like mine in a way I never even imagined it could.

Will that always be true? Who knows. What matters is that I made a commitment to act in line with my true self and in a way that relieved my suffering. That commitment also removed a constant source of churning doubt and worry (*should I should I should I, but what if . . .*). Making the choice and committing to it allowed me to move another step deeper in my journey of self-understanding and gave me more mental and emotional space to serve others.

That is the true meaning of committing to a practice. It's not based on knowledge of the future. No one knows the future, not even how you yourself will feel there. Choosing and committing to a practice requires understanding where you are right now and what choice will take you perhaps a single step more in the direction you think you should go. The real meaning of that commitment is only accessible after you've made it. Sometimes it will be hard as hell to live with. At other times, it will feel like eating your favorite ice cream on a hot day.

Living with it and letting it change you and watching your own reaction to that change is yoga, it's *svadhyaya*, and it's also transness.

The lesson the *Sutras* offer here is timeless and has nothing whatsoever to do with whether you do Downward Facing Dog or meditation or drink caffeine or get tattoos. The lesson is that a personal, *staggering*, life-changing experience is available to you, but you can only get there by choosing to practice, by being earnest and committed in that practice, and by allowing yourself to observe what happens when you do.

Someday, if I'm lucky, I will be an eighty-year old with sagging top surgery scars and a bunch of wrinkly old tattoos. Perhaps I'll think about other choices I could have made. But however life marks me between now and then, I will never regret committing wholeheartedly to the practice of uncovering and living as my true self, whatever that might turn out to be.

**I practice every day by asking,
"What am I committed to?
How will I demonstrate my devotion
and earnestness to those commitments?
What will I run toward as if it were a cool treat on a
hot day? How will I observe my reactions to those
commitments and allow myself to be transformed by
them?"**

Chapter 3
Clearing the Brush

I HIT MYSELF FOR THE FIRST TIME WHEN I WAS SIX. I'M NOT going to go into all the reasons why I did that, but I will say that it's the first time I consciously remember wishing I were someone else. Not anyone else in particular, just not *me*. When there are large and important parts of a child's experience that they know cannot be acknowledged, when there is no one to share them with and a pervasive fear that speaking them aloud will be dangerous in some as-yet-not-understood way, that child will find a way to survive.

I remember that first time as clearly as I remember this morning, sometimes more so. I was standing in front of the mirror in the room I shared with my sister. I remember how the morning light slanted in through the window. I also remember the feeling that I was alone. Not just that there was no one else in the house, but no one else in the universe. No one to speak to, or share with, or cry out for.

Looking back as an adult, I know, intellectually, that there must have been someone else in the house, but children know things on a feeling level, below and above rational logic. I knew that there was no one I could reach for. Whether an adult happened to be sitting in another room didn't change that.

As I looked in the mirror, a feeling started to build in my gut. Something between rage and hopelessness. In the same way I knew I was alone, I also knew that I *could not let this thing out*. It was one of the things that was not allowed.

So quick as a thought, much more quickly than I can tell or even remember it, I hit myself, as hard as I could, with my wood-handled hairbrush, *onetwothreefourfive!* I don't remember whether the words "shut up shut up shut up" actually went through my mind at the time, but that's the feeling that went with the motion.

I hit myself so hard I had to put a hand out to the wall to stay upright. The room swam around me. I was horrified . . . and . . . in a secret part of myself, I was also exalted by the power of it. I was no longer completely helpless. I had the ability to control this over-whelming thing inside me.

So began four decades of self harm.

When I was twelve, I tried to kill myself. Not very effectively, but effectively enough to call attention to myself, which was a very bad idea. I was sent to a locked psychiatric ward for children. When I was being "evaluated" for admission, or I should say, when the psychiatrist spoke with my parents while I sat off to the side, already learning to not exist, I was offered a choice. They said, essentially, that either I was lying about wanting to kill myself, or I was dangerous and had to be locked up.

Liar? Or dangerous? Or both? My weeks on the locked ward gave that question time to worm itself deep into my psyche. The first night, lying on the floor of the lobby under the bored gaze of an orderly (I was on suicide watch and couldn't be allowed to sleep in a bed), I truly began to separate myself into pieces, some in control of surviving and others, suppressed further and further down where they couldn't show their dangerous little heads, locked into feelings and memories I could not speak.

My parents ran true to form in never speaking of my experience on that ward, ever. They never asked me a question about it or wanted to know. Not wanting to know is something they share in common. Not acknowledging reality is how they themselves learned to survive. The only mention of that ward from the moment I got home until thirty years later was a threat, whenever I started to get "out of hand" again: "Do we have to send you back?"

Lord god almighty no. And so I punched, and starved, and strangled, and whipped, and burned, and cut myself to keep down all the things we weren't acknowledging. The memories and feelings underneath got more and more outside of consciousness, leaving the rigid self-control and the occasional violence it required. Long after I moved out, some deep and powerful part of my brain still told me, "Keep quiet, you fool, or you'll be incarcerated, exiled, tortured."

If you don't believe torture is the right word, allow me to gift you the image, seen down a long, dark hallway, of a young girl screaming and screaming and screaming, tied with leather straps to her bed because she kicked in the glass door to the group room —because her parents brought along to visiting hours the uncle who had molested her for years, to prove to her that she was lying. That wasn't me, but she lives and lives and screams and screams in my mind still.

Or the five year old boy whose life at home was so unendurable that he tried to kill himself by stabbing himself in the eye.

I won't go on. There's no need. Suffice it to say that, when we get to the discussions about the yogic concept of suffering, which is a lot of what the *Sutras* are about, it's not just theoretical for me. I didn't need a book to tell me that suffering was inherent in the nature of this human existence.

I also won't get into running away from home years later, or being arrested, or any of the other slimy things that swam unresolved in the deep parts of my mind as I grew into adulthood.

As I said, I discovered yoga just after college. It helped. I kept practicing. I practiced and practiced. I completed my first teacher training. Feeling excited to go deeper, I signed up for a Tantric meditation course.

I believed at the time that the *Sutras* insisted on a particular type of meditation as the Only Path to true peace and liberation. The course I signed up for offered to teach traditional powerful forms of meditation that would allow us to access mindstates more blissful and freeing than any we had achieved in our previous practices. I was *thrilled*.

I was also not. Not. Not. NOT. Ready.

Going deep into the inner psyche while it is still swimming with unacknowledged, unprocessed monsters is a dangerous game. But all too often, yoga practices like these are taught alongside messages that tell you that if you can't achieve deep meditation, it's because you're not trying hard enough or doing it right, or perhaps yoga just isn't "right" for you. Your unreadiness is framed as a moral problem or a pathology rather than an understanding of the necessary steps for deepening a practice.

Research tells us, now, that attempting to directly access the mind, to attempt to still its fluctuations by diving inward in meditation, with unprocessed trauma or active PTSD, can be a very bad idea. Your mind has locked certain experiences into lead-lined vaults for a reason. They need to be opened, examined, and dealt with, but not by throwing all the lids wide all at once in an unprotected space.

It has been argued, in fact, that nothing in the entire *Yoga Sutras* is for beginners at all. The eight steps (a series of practices laid out by Patanjali that we'll talk about in a minute) "are really advanced techniques," according to Swami Satyananda Saraswati, "for those people who have exhausted most of their mental problems and conflicts." For many people, these practices would "do more harm than good," he says. The Tantric meditation class was my visceral education in the truth of that statement.

Before beginning our transformational quest in earnest, we have to do what I call clearing the brush. If Patanjali's *Sutras* are a syllabus, clearing the brush is the prerequisite. On our quest, clearing the brush is everything we must do before we're ready to set out.

Preparing the Soil

When he was thirteen or fourteen, my brother took on the task of weedeating the overgrown back yard of our new house. I don't think anyone had maintained it in years. Waist-high, snarled grasses and weeds choked each other under the shadow of over-hanging trees, and who knows what might have been lurking beneath.

Well, we know one thing: poison oak.

My brother took the weedeater to the entire patch of ground, essentially hurling pellets of poison oak at himself at twenty miles an hour. The resulting sores were like chicken pox, runny and red and, judging from his expression, unbearably itchy. He lived in calamine lotion for the next week.

Before we can get down to the subtleties of inner liberation, we have to clear the weeds and tangled vines that keep us from accessing it. You wouldn't just throw your vegetable seeds into that thicket of who-knows-what and hope they could grow in the suffo-cating spaces between the weeds. You would clear the ground.

Like my brother, though, we need to be careful as we begin this process. When I threw myself into a deeper meditation prac-tice than I was ready for, I experienced the equivalent of poison oak sores. I had nightmares and panic attacks. I began to experi-ence anger—*rage*, actually—without knowing why. I began hurting myself again after a period of respite. Because I didn't know what was causing these problems, I assumed (as I usually do) that it must be my fault. I was doing it wrong. I wasn't "yoga" enough.

I doubled down and practiced harder, trying to force my anger away with deep breathing and avoiding panic attacks and fear by never, ever allowing a moment in which I wasn't doing anything.

Finally, it got so bad that I decided to try therapy. Thanks to my experience on the psych ward as a child, I didn't exactly believe in therapy. But my anger and anxiety and hurt were thrashing me around in so many directions, it was like I was tied to the bull. It felt like my only way off was to cut the rope holding me on. To kill myself.

Somehow, I found Tracy. We stepped all the way back to the beginning by creating safety. I wanted to hurl myself into the deep end like I always do, and she helped me moderate my pace and develop a foundation under myself first. I was astounded by how much I needed to work through and frustrated by how long the process seemed to take.

That was not the beginning of clearing the brush for me, though. Surprising as it might sound, the beginning was when I hit myself for the first time. My six-year-old self believed that it was that or literally die, and I somehow chose to survive, as so many children do. One small choice of the lesser harm.

At each inflection point in a person's life, every moment of choice, every opportunity to step this way . . . or *that* way . . . we meet this same potential for the lesser harm. The slightly better good. Each time we choose in that direction, we are clearing the brush.

Next time, wear a long-sleeved shirt when you weed-eat the garden. Then perhaps a weekly mowing instead of letting it get so bad. Then daily watering and weeding. A simple practice of movement toward less-suffering that adds up to a complete and total change in your experience of life.

Sri Satchidananda offers an analogy for this that I adore. He compares clearing the mind to cleaning out a closet. Eventually, maybe we'll get rid of everything, but "before we come to that, it makes it easier to dispose of them if we sort them first. Why? Because we still have a little clinging. We can't just throw everything away so easily." Our mental wardrobe gets full of stuff we don't need, including parts that are harmful to us, and by choosing to practice, we are committing to sort through and let go of the parts we don't need. But we don't want to get rid of everything all at once. Not even all the potentially harmful stuff.

As my therapist put it, "It's not necessarily a good idea to get rid of all your coping mechanisms at once."

Satchidananda continues the analogy: "You may say, 'I'll give these away to somebody.' But by the time you take it to the door, your mind will say, 'I think I should keep just this one.'" We can use this to our advantage. "Your mental wardrobe is also full. You want to throw something out, but you don't feel like just dumping out everything." We feel more comfortable when we only give up what we can part with at any given moment. Taking this approach feels much more manageable, and much more realistic, than attempting to achieve mental stillness straight off the couch.

A lot of this cleaning out process happens before you do anything the world calls "yoga," but it's an indispensable part of the practice nonetheless. In fact, given that almost all of us will stay in this process our whole lives, it might be the most important practice of all.

Outside In

At some point in my life, I went from actively starving myself and making myself throw up, to exercising obsessively and rigidly controlling what I ate. From there, I went down a rabbit hole of nutrition and exercise science as a way to control my body (a form of health perfectionism known as orthorexia). Not great—but better than what I'd been doing before.

That obsession also led me to deepen my physical yoga practice. I became a strict vegan and then, eventually, found that I actually needed to be less strict with my diet in the name of better health. For a long time, I ate the same foods, repeatedly, every single day and practiced power yoga as often as I could find a class. At the time, I believed this was the pinnacle of wellbeing. And for me, at that moment, it *was*. We can only practice where we are, and every choice toward a slightly more aligned and liberated self moved me in the direction I needed to be going, even when I didn't know what direction that was.

Once I started therapy, my pattern of self-controlling perfectionism showed itself in its true forms: shame, self-loathing, and a backassward form of protection that probably saved my life as a child but was now stealing my energy and my capacity to live my life in the present.

From there, I began to practice loosening. Opening up. That's where I am now. Sharing my story with you is one piece of opening myself to the world and allowing myself to believe that maybe it is safe to live a full life.

Every part of this multiple-decade journey has been necessary, given where I started and the resources I had available at each step. For nearly one entire year, quitting smoking dominated my practice. I smoked less, and then less, and now it's been years. Hating myself every time I smoked a cigarette wasn't helpful. The practice of noticing how I felt—how I *really* felt—when I was smoking versus when I wasn't, and choosing more and more often to move toward the freedom of giving it up, worked.

For many, many people I know, sobriety is a necessary element of clearing the brush, often the first. It can take years, and it has its own progression of clearing something out of the way and then going deeper and then clearing away the next thing that comes up.

Coming out as queer in some form, maybe more than once, to many people, over the course of months or years, can be part of clearing the brush, too.

Think about what you will need to feel ready to set out on the quest for self-realization. Perhaps there are relationships that cause so much conflict or anxiety that you simply cannot imagine having the time or energy to practice. If so, now is the time to step back and figure out how to resolve them, whether that's creating space and boundaries or directly addressing an unspoken issue between you. Perhaps your financial situation is so difficult that, again, the idea of self-realization feels utterly out of reach. Until that's dealt with, it will be almost impossible to truly commit to your quest.

Clearing the brush might mean creating a budget and climbing your way out from under the psychic burden of debt. As I found myself, clearing the brush often includes therapy and trauma processing before deeper spiritual work can even begin. Get your relationships right, build a foundation of security under yourself to the best of your ability, release yourself from the mental gymnastics involved in lying.

None of these tasks are easy. Often, something must be given up. I recently watched *Hedwig and the Angry Inch* again and was struck by Hedwig's mother saying that sometimes, in order to walk away, you have to leave a piece of yourself behind. I know I have, many times. You can begin to see why commitment and devotion are so important. It's not that we wouldn't finish the quest without them; it's that we would probably never even begin.

What all the tasks of clearing the brush have in common is that they move us from the outside in: from the big obvious stuff that's messing up our lives to the smaller and less visible patterns that lie beneath. We can't plant the garden until that tangle of poison oak is removed.

The *Sutras* describe five sheaths, or *koshas*, that make up a whole person in yogic philosophy: the physical layer on the outside, the energetic or breath layer just within that, and then, increasingly subtle, the mental, intuitive, and finally blissful layers. The blissful *kosha* is the unvarnished self, without any of the other layers wrapped like onion skins around it. To reach it requires peeling back those other skins to reveal the inner light with less and less obstruction.

The eventual goal is to transcend all of these *koshas*, moving gradually from gross to subtle. The key word is *eventually*. The starting point isn't to jump into intense meditation and just "transcend" all the other stuff in your life like it doesn't exist.

Patanajali offers a workbook for this outside-in practice called the eight-fold path. It's the focus of the second section of the *Sutras*, the "portion on practice." The lesson of the eight-fold path is: do the big work first. Free yourself, as much as you can, from the raging bull instead of trying to meditate in the saddle.

The eight-fold path therefore does not start with meditation or enlightenment or even physical practice. It begins with ten ethical rules, grouped into two categories: the *yamas* and the *niyamas*. The *yamas* are guides for living in the world, and the *niyamas* are guides for living with ourselves. Already, you can see the pattern of moving from the outside in.

The *yamas* and *niyamas* make up an entire practice in themselves, from *satya* (truthfulness) and *asteya* (not stealing) to *santosha* (contentment) and *saucha* (cleanliness). Like Gandhi and Hanuman, we could take *ahimsa* or *brahmacharya* as the whole of a life's work. The lesson of the *yamas* and *niyamas* is in fact deeply practical and based in human psychology and experience. It's not so much that we have to practice this or that exact "austerity" or ethical behavior. Patanjali's insight is that we're going to have a heck of a hard time pursuing deeper spiritual practices of any kind when our outer experience and behavior don't match our inner purpose.

I'm not going to go into depth on each of the ten here, especially given the extreme variations in translation and interpretation around each of them. I've listed some incredible books about the *yamas* and *niyamas* in the references section if you want to dive into them. I want to focus instead on the effect or purpose of these guidelines. Sri Saraswati tells us that "they tackle the problem of mental disturbance from the outer edge, the periphery," and in doing that, they are "a start to more profound changes." In that sense, they offer a map to the work of clearing the brush.

After we make these big-picture shifts in how we live with ourselves and others, we find our way to *asana*, the third element of the eight-fold path. In the *Sutras*, *asana* is anything that helps us find our "secure seat." It's often interpreted as physical practice, but a better term might be physical preparation. Just as it's hard to practice while we're living in emotional turmoil, we can also be held back by physical discomfort. Physical practices that build our capacity to sit, to concentrate, and to be aware of our internal experience are all part of *asana*. Much of what we now know as *asana* comes from the *hatha* tradition, which is mentioned by most of the *Sutra* translations as excellent preparation for the "royal road." It's like the training montage in a physical quest movie, except that instead of preparing ourselves for an outward quest, we are preparing our minds and bodies for the quest within. Just as with a physical quest, the inward journey requires strength and discipline.

The other five limbs of the eightfold path continue in this way, becoming increasing subtle: from breathwork to concentration and finally to *samadhi*, our final aim.

The big, tangled emotional weeds keeping us enmeshed need to be cleared away first. If you've been embezzling, stop. If you feel agitation every day because of discontent with your job, deal with that first. If you are in an unsafe situation, please find resources and help to get out of that rather than focusing your attention on "living with it" by seeking nonattachment. I speak from experience and love when I say this. We only have so much energy and capacity. The journey is long. Preparing adequately might feel slow, but it is the only way to make it to the end.

Much of the basic hygiene of living can function as clearing the brush. I say "basic," but keeping my space clean, paying my bills on time, shopping for groceries and preparing food, and washing my clothes and putting them away before they became a wrinkled mess took me years to get a handle on. The tide only turned when I experienced for myself how different I felt when I made an effort on one of these items. That turned into a bigger effort and finally became a habit and then an intentional practice.

Clearing the brush is often a literal process of creating space for ourselves. When I stopped hunching over my laptop and bought myself an honest-to-god adult desk, my writing practice was transformed. I was in my forties. It turned out that my inability to believe that I needed a desk was tied up with all kinds of subtler issues around what I deserve and whether my writing counted as real work, even as I supported myself with it for years.

With each obstacle removed, subtler ones are revealed beneath, and so our practice continues.

There's a tendency to read the eight limbs, and especially the *yamas and niyamas*, as religious rules. I can't stress enough that this process is a psychological and pragmatic one, not a moral one. Patanjali is telling us, *hey, spiritual work is hard—don't make it any harder than it has to be. Get your house in order first, as much as you can.*

Obviously, in our culture, not everyone has equal access to stability. I don't believe that "not lying" means I have to trumpet to everyone in my vicinity that I'm trans, especially in places where I don't feel safe. My mother was born with spina bifida. For her and others living with disabilities, complete freedom from physical pain, or the achievement of a "comfortable seat" for meditation, may not be reasonable goals. Contentment is easier to reach for when you're not living with PTSD or inhabiting a racialized identity.

Patanjali is asking us to identify what we can do for ourselves and do it. He is also reminding us that part of our work is to clear the brush on a larger scale. Poison oak lies much thicker around some homes in our society than others. Clearing the brush is a community action as well as a personal one, ensuring that *all* people have the ability to pursue spiritual work if they choose. In this sense, Patanjali's philosophy is not only compatible with social justice work; it requires it.

Courageous people have found deep spiritual practices in the absolute worst conditions imaginable, for as long as humans have existed. Their stories are inspiration for all of us. But I think that sometimes we hold up these extraordinary humans and believe that our own practice has to be just as hard, or is less meaningful if it isn't—that yoga is about *endurance.* It is not. Those things we have to endure, we have to endure. But we are allowed, indeed encouraged, to remove whatever suffering we can.

Crashing Toward Enlightenment

One of the symptoms of my PTSD is sensitivity to sound. And when I say sensitivity to sound, I don't mean a polite, "Could you turn that down?" or putting my fingers in my ears. I mean instant, life-altering rage. I'll be going along, living my life, feeling pretty okay, and I'll hear some particular triggering sound, like my downstairs neighbors slamming their doors, and my body will scream immediately into the red.

It's like waking up out of a deep sleep at the wheel of a car going 100 miles an hour. Imagine what you would do in that situation. Probably freak the fuck out. I don't generally swear, but I think it's warranted here because I don't know how else to describe the nuclear-sized reaction of fear and chaos that I experience in these situations.

When you wake up at the wheel of a car going 100, what happens is that you freak out, and then everything goes spectacularly wrong in pretty predictable ways. You scream, thrash, become frantic, feel like you're about to die, or rather *know* you are about to die—and then crash. For me, in the past, the worst of these crashes have involved anger and then shame at my anger and then self-loathing self-harm or suicide attempts.

There's no rationality to it. My body is one thousand percent certain it is about to die, and every system goes into red-alert, overload, all-or-nothing reaction mode.

From the outside, especially if the noise has already stopped or is relatively minor, this looks insane. Part of me is aware that it's gotten quiet again, that I can hear birds through the open window, and that I am not currently dying. But the train has already left the station. The car is already going 100.

At other times, in the depths of grief after my divorce, for example, I've found myself at the other end of the energy spectrum, lying in bed in the middle of the day, not even sure how I ended up there, physically unable to lift my head to look at the clock. That deathlike exhaustion can feel as uncontrollable and as likely to destroy my life as the rage.

Yoga has names for these two states: *rajasic* and *tamasic*. I call them "can't stop" and "can't get going," or *revved-up* and *lethargic*. Whatever you call them, they're key terms for developing a practice of clearing the brush. All of us can experience both of these states, often in the course of the same day, although thankfully not always as intensely as I've described them here. Each of us also tends toward one more than the other. I tend to be *rajasic*: I'm much more often over-revved than unable to start.

They're also not bad or evil. When I'm revved up, yes, I'm more likely to get into extreme fight-or-flight mode, but I'm also more productive and have more ideas. When I'm *tamasic*, I feel less productive, but I also let myself rest and recover.

The middle ground is a lovely place called *sattva*, or experiencing *sattvic* energy. It's a balanced point between too-up and too-down, too fast and too slow. The Goldilocks energy. *Sattva* is another of Patanjali's "Nobel Prize" descriptions. The ultimate prize would be to find ourselves in *sattva* all the time, but getting there is a life-long journey. Trying to push yourself into a *sattvic* state, or performing as if you're in one when you're not, is a setup for problems.

When I'm super revved-up, hypervigilant and amped so high my body feels like it's going to have to physically expand to contain all this energy, going directly into deep breathing or other "calming" exercises is like trying to stop your car by driving it directly into a wall. Yes, it will probably stop, but there is going to be some damage. For me, that damage is the painful muscle cramps and racing mind that come from trying to stuff all that red-hot energy into a seated body.

Clearing the brush on a daily or even moment-to-moment basis includes being aware of your *rajasic* or *tamasic* energy and engaging with it. When I'm in nuclear mode, I will sometimes throw my shoes on and go out for a sprint. Not a run, an all-out *sprint*, literally running for my life. As it turns out, you don't have to sprint very far at top speed to wear out a lot of that energy.

From there, I work inward. Maybe I listen to hard, loud, angry music while I'm sprinting. Then, as the energy dissipates, I switch to running slower and listening to music that's still a bit hard and fast, but maybe more positive and upbeat. Slower and slower, less angry, less reactive. Sometimes I get all the way back to baseline (hallelujiah!). Other days, I can only contain it enough to get through the rest of the day without physically tearing myself apart. Either way, the work of clearing the brush—starting where I am, from the outside in, and dealing with the big, obvious stuff first—

makes it possible for me to approach the deeper and subtler practices, if that's in the cards for today.

The same pattern holds true over a lifetime. The first time you wake up in a car going 100 miles an hour, yes, you freak out, scream, and crash. And the second time. And the third time. That's going to keep happening for a while because it's not an experience you get used to easily. Over time, though, you become just experienced enough with waking up in a speeding vehicle to be able to look around and say, "Huh, this seems familiar," right before you crash.

That period of waking, rational self-awareness, if cultivated, can grow longer and longer.

After a while, you might find yourself more annoyed than anything ("this again!!"). You start to carry mental protocols called "what to do when you wake up in a car going 100." There are times when it feels massively unfair that no one else seems to be taking up brain space with a full-length user's manual for what to do when you wake up in a car going 100 miles an hour, but the first time you're able to completely stop yourself before you cause emotional or physical damage, it becomes worth all the effort.

Over the years I've practiced these protocols, I've become less reactive to noise in general. Fewer noises set the car revving. The feeling of being out of control happens less often and doesn't last as long. There are days it barely happens at all.

For those of you who are sober, this might sound familiar. In a sense, we are addicted to the mental states we're used to, even when they are killing us. As a highly *rajasic* person, the patience required to continue this work over weeks and months and years has sometimes been almost impossible. But not, in the end, actually impossible.

Over time, we adjust whatever we can in the direction of greater psychological safety and lower emotional turmoil. We clear away the large brush so that we can see the path more clearly.

Who knows? Maybe the path you find will be the path of yoga, even if that wasn't your original intent.

Transforming

When I told my brother I was trans, he was surprised. He knew that a lot of the expectations about being female didn't sit right with me, but to him, that didn't suggest that I wanted to be something else.

"Every woman I know is slightly uncomfortable all the time," he said, "I guess I just thought it was that."

I don't know whether all women feel uncomfortable all the time (although what a damning statement about being female in this culture if it's even remotely true), but I do know that I was uncomfortable—itchingly, painfully, wretchedly uncomfortable—literally all the time.

Almost the first thing my mother did after I was born was to start taping pink bows to my head so that people would "know I was a girl." According to her, I didn't have enough hair to signal this all-important distinction, possibly because I was born premature. That I was already massively uncomfortable in my body (gendered or otherwise) is clear from the fact that I wouldn't eat. I was a projectile-vomiter, unable to keep down enough calories to grow properly for a long time after I was born.

Somehow, the insistence on femaleness and this gut-level physical discomfort came to be blended.

I have a notebook my mother started when I was born. She wrote, "Your father can't believe he was involved in making something female." I can understand, on some level, the awe that was probably intended behind that statement. All I can say is, by the time I read those words, they conveyed something very different to me, because in addition to the the pink bows, my mother got my ears pierced when I was six months old, just in case the bows weren't conveying the idea. And then there were the dresses. My mother is a master-level seamstress, embroider, and knitter. She makes pieces that could be shown in museums, if museums were interested in showing that kind of thing. She would design and make for me (and later my sister as well) ornate, museum-worthy pieces that made me hate my existence. Itchy, scratchy, girly, puffy, pink and white, stiff with embroidery and lace, like Renaissance gowns or Victorian visiting costumes.

There's a photo of me, posed in front of a two-winged mirror, my scowling face reflected into infinity, holding a nearly-bald, hideous doll and wearing what felt to me like a two-foot high, floppy, lacy, stiff, embroidered pink hat. My hatred of the thing is expressed in every line of my rigid, furious little body.

There's another photo of me roller-skating off of a table in my orange plastic clip-on Fisher Price roller skates, wearing nothing but Wonder Woman underwear, so it wasn't all femaleness per se that bothered me, although I do wonder what I would have chosen if I'd had all the choices. But from an extremely young age, all the culturally accepted trappings of femininity were anathema to me. When older ladies at church would tell me, *Oh, what a pretty little girl!* I would hurl myself face-first to the ground and yell, *NO, I'm NOT.*

I stand by that.

When I tell people about my history, they often assume that my mother's obsession with a particular 1950s version of femaleness somehow made me trans, but that's not how it works. Transness is present in my earliest memories, long before I had a word for it. Transness is just a thing about me, like blue eyes.

I can't remember exactly the first time I thought, "People will be mad if I go into the girls' bathroom because they can *tell* I'm a boy," but I can't have been more than five or six. I kept waiting for my boy part to grow in. I wanted to wear boy clothes and play on the boys' teams and be friends with the boys.

But my brother is also right: many, many girls and women are uncomfortable with the expectations around performing femaleness in our society. There are tomboys and butches and so-called "masculine" women of every stripe, as well as feminine women who don't always love the performance, no matter how good at it they are.

Like many of them, I also feel the frustration, anger, irritation, annoyance, and discomfort associated with being read as female in a misogynistic culture. I lived, worked, dated, got married and divorced, managed corporate jobs, got paid (or not), and had to maneuver around existing structures as a woman for *decades*. I have nothing but empathy for, and solidarity with, people who want to change the ways that women are seen and their experience in the world. Their discomfort is information, too—for all of us.

When I finally started to ask myself, "Am I trans?," all these aspects of my experience were tangled up together like yarn left too long in a drawer. I spent months going back and forth in my own mind, with my friends, with my therapist, with anyone who would listen.

Yes, transness offers me freedom from gendered expectations, and discovering my nonbinary-ish middle ground doubly so.

And no, the desire to be free from those expectations isn't in itself transness, nor did it "make" me trans.

Yes, my mother's complex feelings about femaleness got worked out through me, perhaps especially the complexity of her feelings of being denied access to certain validations of her femaleness because of her disability. Yes, I can both feel compassion for her struggle and recognize its painful influence on my ability to live as myself.

And no, none of that made me trans. I know far too many women with similar experiences who never once, ever, considered the possibility that they might be boys, or nonbinary, or not women.

Yes, I wanted to play with "boy" toys and wear "boy" clothes and do "boy" things.

And no, that isn't transness either. All kids should be allowed to pick out their clothes. The day I found myself unable to keep up with my big brother and his friends because my mother had made me wear an ankle-length skirt is burned in my memory, but experiences like that are common to all kinds of restrictions and unwanted choices.

Yes, I experienced childhood sexual trauma. Yes, that caused dissociation from my body in its own ways. No, that didn't somehow make me trans. That, too, is far too common among people who have no problem defining themselves as the gender they were born with. And believe it or not, there are plenty of trans people who have experienced none of what I've described here.

This melding-together of experiences that are common to many people with experiences that point specifically to transness is what makes it so difficult for trans people to identify themselves. I *agonized* over these questions. *What if I could just be more butch, more masculine? What if I'm mistaken? What if I'm confusing feminism with transness? What if transness is anti-feminist?* And on and on and on.

I sat with these tangled threads for a long time, especially when I was making the decision to pursue so-called medical transition. That was when I truly began to understand what clearing the brush meant. I could not make the decision to commit to medical transition until I cleared away everything that was bound up with transness in my mind, but was not transness.

Any major decision or commitment, including a commitment to a personal or spiritual practice, requires us to untangle our motivations and all the thoughts and experiences we bring to it. Which feelings are our own, and which are the expectations that have been handed to us? Where is your own joy, and what are you performing for others? There's no rule that you have to give up your performances or reject all outside expectations. While you live in the world, that's probably impossible anyway.

The key is knowing the difference. Much of our quest for self-realization will involve untangling ourselves from everything that is *not* the true self. Clearing the brush is the first step, whether that means physically cleaning your space or clearing away the burden of debts (emotional or financial or otherwise), or letting go of habits that served you once but are now harming you. Perhaps you begin to eat a little healthier so you have more energy available for practice. Or maybe, like me, you need to untangle the knotted ball of threads in your head so you can lay out each of the strands and see your way forward more clearly.

I'll leave you with one last thought about clearing the brush: if this is as far as you ever get in your practice, well done to you. A lifetime could be much worse spent. As Swami Saraswati says, "Even limited application will lead to greater peace of mind." The benefits you will see might draw you into deeper practices of self-awareness, or maybe they won't. Either way, clearing away what isn't what you want in your life, and what isn't bringing you joy or moving you in the right direction, is life-altering in itself.

> **I don't ask "is this yoga, or is this not yoga?"**
> **I wonder, "What needs to be cleared away**
> **before I can see my way forward?**
> **What brush is growing over the garden**
> **I want to cultivate?**
> **What must I do to be prepared**
> **for the inner quest ahead?"**

Chapter 4
Impermanence

IN THE VERY HEART OF MY HEART, I BELIEVED MY HUSBAND was my soul mate.

We met for the first time when I was twelve. I was in the back seat of our family's minivan. He was sitting with my older brother in the seat in front of me. They were doing a project together for history class, and I had to ride along. I didn't think, "There's my future husband." I thought, "Ugh, why do I have to be here?"

We started dating when I was sixteen. We each went to prom with someone else, and we ended up together. We got married when I was 21. When we got married, young as we were, we scorned to say, "Till death do us part." We said, "forever"—although, when we talked about it, he did say that he would almost certainly get married again if I died. I tried not to think about that. I was equally certain that I would not. My entire world was constructed around our relationship. It was the one permanent thing I could hold on to.

We got divorced when I was 42. We'd been together for nearly 27 years.

If you have ever gotten divorced, perhaps you will understand the years of bargaining, begging, realizing it wasn't working, and trying again—the desperation—that I went through before I finally wrenched myself away. We had been together for so long, from such a young age, and I had believed so implicitly in our story of ourselves as soul mates, that to imagine any other life felt utterly impossible. Not just sad or hard, but nonexistent. There was no other version of "me" than the one I had shaped around him.

I was as fixed in that relationship as it is possible to be. It defined my sense of self and my identity. I had moored all my career decisions, choices about where and how to live, and relationships with friends and family around this central anchoring point. I've heard divorce described as tearing a tree out by its roots. This felt more like attempting to pull myself out of a black hole when I'd already passed the event horizon. The gravity was so heavy I believed I would rather die than attempt to climb out.

I'm a very determined person, so I refused to believe the door could be closing on a connection that had shaped my entire adult life. Every day, I tried to force it back to the way it used to be, and every day I grew more exhausted and more unhappy. In the end, I did have to nearly die to convince myself that I had to leave. There is still a hole in my life in the shape of him, although it gets smaller as I rebuild myself around my own heart. Loving him and being with him were so imbued into my life that even now, sometimes, it feels like he is part of the trees and the air and all the things I love in the world. Losing him wounded me to the core of my devoted heart.

But my forever relationship was not forever after all. And that, Patanjali tells us, is the nature of everything we encounter in this world.

The *Upanishads*, a collection of early texts that laid out the basic philosophies that were later codified as yoga, refer to "the knots in the heart" by which we tie ourselves to things that are impermanent. What a beautiful and heartbreaking image. It also reminds me why we forge deep connections, even with things we know won't last. We don't tie ourselves to impermanent things because we are stupid or not spiritual enough. We do it because our hearts are designed to form connection.

The concept of impermanence is foundational to the *Yoga Sutras*, but I believe it is often misunderstood as a call to reject the world, to cut through the knots in the heart and float away from life. As I have gone through the many transitions in my life, including gender transition and my transition out of my marriage and into a life centered along my own path, I have discovered another word that has helped me make clearer sense of impermanence. That word is *fluidity*.

For a long time leading up to my divorce, I kept asking myself, "How could something that once gave me so much joy now be causing me such unendurable pain?" How could the boy, the young man, the partner, the husband who took me hiking on our first date and lived with me and held my hand when our rabbit had to be put down and led me up mountains and followed me across the country—how could he now be the chain binding me to suffering? How could my own needs now be so different that I needed to forge away onto my own path, without him? The knot had become a double bind, cutting into my life so tightly that I could not breathe.

Later, I went through a period when I was ashamed of how hurt I was and how much I was grieving. How could I still love him? How could I have been so stupid as to let him treat me that way for so long? I was still tying myself to the past, trying to force it to make sense for me.

I am still grieving his loss, but I'm no longer ashamed to have loved him, and *that* is the lesson of impermanence. Not to give up all of our connections to life, but to acknowledge that as humans, we do become connected, despite knowing that such connections are impermanent.

To allow the knot to unfurl when the connection is done is the other half of love.

You Are Still Here

Impermanence isn't only a yogic idea. It was also one of the first concepts gifted to me by my therapist. She sent me a book chapter titled something like "No Feeling is Forever." At the time, I was in a period of self-harming that was part of my attempt to do *anything* rather than leave my known life and start over. It seemed that if I could just locate the problem in myself, maybe I could punish it away. The panicked brain is not rational, but it has a logic of its own that can be very compelling when it aligns with our desire not to change.

I read the chapter she sent me, and I *railed* against it. I was furious with it. How dare it suggest that my love for my partner wouldn't last forever? Or that my anger, my hurt, my grief were passing experiences? It seemed to be saying that these feelings were unimportant or not real because they would eventually pass. The fact that I would not grieve every moment for the rest of my life seemed to suggest that my marriage had been a sham, that it had never meant what I thought it meant.

I was grieving my own fixation, my sense of being fixed in place. I had complained about being stuck, and I was, but stuck is also another word for connected.

Even at the time, I think I knew that I was angry because it was true. My feelings would not last forever. I could leave that life. I could build a new one. I could find another kind of joy, another shape for my future. The lesson I didn't want to learn was this one: "When something changes, it can't be the Self."

"Temporarily keep things," says Sri Satchidananda, "but know that you are a trustee, not an owner . . . Once something has ripened, it should be passed on." And again later: "Changes are like running water. If you just allow water to flow, it is very pleasant to sit and watch. But if you want to arrest the flow and keep the water for yourself, you will have to construct a dam. Then the water will resist the dam and try to escape. There will be a terrible struggle."

Terrible struggle certainly describes how I felt during my divorce.

By the way, the people who tell you, "You're better off without him!" or "There are other fish in the sea!" aren't embracing impermanence. They are trying to soothe their own fears by making yours go away. To understand impermanence, you have to understand the difference, not just between impermanent and permanent, but between permanent and *real*.

My love for my husband and my joy in that relationship weren't permanent, but they were very real. That's what makes letting go of them so difficult. In order to heal, I had to accept not only the impermanence but also the reality of my love for my husband, the reality of the ties and binds between us that were not all shackles, the reality of the pain that was required to move into something else. It would actually be easier to believe that the entire visible and sensory world is fake, a dream. Its reality is what makes it painful, and what allows it to touch us.

It has been some time now since my divorce. I look different. I feel different. I grieve what I lost, but I am still here.

During my gender transition, my name changed, my face changed, my body changed, my *smell* changed, the way I was perceived and understood in the world changed. My rights changed. But I am still here.

Who the "I" is that still remains is the question at the heart of this practice, and it's one we can only answer by engaging with the world and having the layers of "not-me" peeled off painfully, one at a time, so we can see what is underneath.

Whatever is left when the struggle has passed, that is the true Self. You survive the wreck. Underneath it all, *you* are still here.

"I Hurt"

Suffering is one of the main themes of the *Sutras*. It's important to understand, though, that suffering is not the same as pain, in the same way that joy is different from pleasure. As the Buddha discovered, it's possible to find tremendous joy in the face of pain, and equally possible to suffer terribly in the midst of every kind of pleasure.

That's not to say that all pleasure is really suffering or that the goal is to never experience pleasure again. It's also not a promise to remove pain. Nor is it an instruction to ignore pain or try to "overcome" it using yoga practices. I've been shocked and grieved to see some yoga students, and even teachers, avoid needed medical care or mental health support because they believed that to be true yogis, they had to cure themselves from within.

The *Sutras* are very clear about the difference. Edwin Bryant uses the analogy of an injured foot: "there are remedies for suffering in the world," he writes. "For example, the sole of the foot is capable of being pierced, and the thorn of piercing it. The remedy is to remove the thorn from the foot (or, better still, not to put the foot on the thorn)." The kind of suffering we experience in the day-to-day world, in our physical, mental, and emotional bodies, is more accurately described as pain or distress. There are, as Bryant says, "remedies" for this kind of pain, and we should use them.

Ayurveda, a "sister science" to yoga, was developed in part to do the work of healing the physical body so that spiritual work could begin. This goes back to clearing the brush: it's hard to practice deeply when we are in physical, psychic, or emotional pain. And so much more of our pain is avoidable now than it was when the *Sutras* were written. We have antibiotics, painkillers, complex surgeries, and all kinds of psychotherapy. It's possible that people in Patanjali's time had access to treatments we've lost. Whatever remedies might be available to you, there is no reason not to avoid pain that can be avoided.

Suffering, on the other hand, is the pain that cannot be avoided, and suffering has not changed one bit since Patanjali's time. It arises out of the core of the human experience: our entanglement with the physical, temporary world and our inability to discriminate between what is permanent and what is not. This core suffering is also called "bondage" because we are tied to the world by the knots in our hearts.

To put it crudely, yoga cannot cure cancer, but it can help you live with it. Yoga cannot erase trauma, but it can help widen your window of tolerance so you can sit with it and heal. Or to use Bryant's analogy, in the same way that we have remedies for the pains of everyday life, yoga is a remedy for the pains that are left, the spiritual and existential pains that medicine cannot touch.

This is not to say that your thoughts create your reality. If anything, the message of the *Sutras* is the exact opposite. They offer a much, much harder lesson: that reality is real. How much easier it would be if our thoughts created our reality! Yes, changing the way we understand a situation can dramatically change our experience of it, no question. But the reality itself remains—and some realities are more stubborn than others. Living in a war zone cannot be wished away. Abuse is not a question of perception. If anything, it is those who wish to abuse you who will most ardently tell you that it's "all in your mind" or that you could overcome remediable physical or environmental causes of distress by "transcending" them.

Patanjali's terms for the permanent and the impermanent are *purusha* and *prakriti*. *Purusha* is the true, abiding, eternal Self, and *prakriti* is everything else. These elements are also called the "seer" and the "seen," or the never-changing and the ever-changing. The true Self is the one who observes the world from within; what is outside our Selves is transient and can simply be observed.

Pain and pleasure are real, but they aren't *us*. To say, "I hurt" doesn't make sense in the worldview of the *Sutras*. The "I" is an eternal, untouchable reality. Your body can hurt. Your mind can be upset or anxious. But you, yourself, are always whole.

The more I practice, the more I feel compassion and love for the body, the mind, the impermanent person to whom I am linked for life. I can step back from them now and see their suffering and say, "I feel for you." Nonetheless, that suffering self is not really me. The sculptor moves the figurines around and keeps them safe, protecting them from breaking and finding a nice spot for them to watch the world from, but he doesn't think he's one of them. He knows that, in the end, they will be molded back into the original ball of clay to form something new.

It's a complicated lesson for someone who has gone to as much trouble as I have to change my physical body.

Fixed

"Fix" has a number of different meanings in English, and each of them offers a key to our quest. We can fix something in the sense of mending what is broken. We can become fixed: cemented in place physically, mentally, or emotionally. To fix can also mean to determine the location of something, as in, "I've got a fix on that missing package." The military uses this meaning to talk about identifying, or nailing down, the location of an opposing force, a target, or incoming support.

The desire to fix a problem is often the reason we start out on a quest in the first place, whether it's the problem of suffering in our own lives or a broader social problem. On the other hand, being fixed, or cemented, in familiarity is just as often what keeps us from starting. And when we become fixed, or want to maintain our own fixtures, we fixate on, or target, others instead. Think of Bilbo Baggins, at the beginning of *The Hobbit*, sitting in his comfortable armchair, rejecting Gandalf's offer for adventure and grumbling about the dwarves messing up his home. Bilbo has spent his entire life desperately craving adventure, but when the opportunity is handed to him, he plants himself in his living room and refuses to budge.

I have a complicated relationship with the concept of fixing. Most of my life, I have been treated as something to be fixed, as in mended or made whole. Something broken. Our culture, on a broad scale, certainly sees trans people this way, whether as victims of faddish groupthink, sufferers with a mental illness, or immoral violators of the natural order.

I have also, sometimes, longed to be fixed, in the sense of finding solid ground. I've longed for the singular sense of self that I perceived others around me to come by naturally. To be fixed in this way is to be cemented, contained. A fixture can be a foundation or a way to hold other things in place. People of all genders want to be correctly identified by the people around them, and trans people are no different. We go to a lot of trouble, all of us, to fix a particular impression of ourselves in other people's minds, whether that has to do with gender or social status or political affiliations.

But the cultural desire to mend trans brokenness goes beyond the individual. It draws on a deeper feeling: the desire for gender itself to be fixed, for gender definitions to be fixtures on which expectations, norms, and rules can be built. Transness is literally the un-fixing of those expectations. The existence of trans, nonbinary, genderqueer, gender fluid, and agender people reveals gender to be much less cemented in place than many people would like.

In a time of massive change and exponentially increasing

complexity, cultures tend to tighten their hold on any fixture they can. AI, social media, globalization, changing demographics: with every added layer of complexity, the desire for something to stay fixed becomes more compulsive. In this climate, the unfixing of gender norms breeds fixations. Politicians fixate on writing out long legal definitions of what "man" and "woman" mean. Communities fixate on who is using which bathroom. Even scientists fixate on identifying a singular cause of transness or a definitive answer about the effects of gender-affirming care.

Ultimately, such fixations take us down a road to the other kind of fixing: targeting. Getting a "fix" on who is reading to children and who gets what healthcare and who is trying to access legal documents become all-important cultural drivers—all in the name of re-fixing, or recementing, strict definitions of gender so that those who stood upon them can continue to feel the illusion of permanence.

The *Sutras* have a word for this kind of fixation: *avidya*. Often translated as "ignorance," the literal meaning derives from the two parts of the word. The prefix *a-*, in Sanskrit as in English, means "not" or "the opposite" (as in asymmetrical). *Vidya* means knowing, or more specifically, correct knowledge gained through discernment. So *avidya* refers to not knowing the underlying truth of something.

When we become fixed, the underlying truth we are not seeing is impermanence. *Avidya* is the inability to tell the difference between that which is permanent or eternal, and that which is impermanent or temporary. "We take the changing appearances to be the unchanging Self," writes Sri Satchidananda. Edwin Bryant, in his overview of the many traditions within the *Sutras*, gives a wonderful list. He writes that *avidya* occurs when we believe that which is "ephemeral" or "fleeting" to be "imperishable," "infinite," "absolute."

Some teachers describe the difference as reality versus appearance, but that is closer to the Buddhist concept of the world. In the *Sutras*, the question isn't about what is real and what isn't real. It's all real.

The suffering we feel when we can't give up our fixations, in particular, is all too real. The ice cream melts. The relationship ends. A person we love dies. Our own lives will end. All of these causes of suffering are absolutely real. That's what makes them so painful.

But let's not forget that the pleasure and meaning we get out of temporary experiences are also real. Practice itself is temporary. A delicious meal is temporary. The perfect day you spent with your partner when you realized you were in love was temporary. One of the great misunderstandings of the *Sutras*, which we will come back to, is that impermanence is the same as unreality, that only permanent things are "real," and that therefore we should give up everything that isn't the eternal Self and remove ourselves from life.

Not so. Satchidananda in particular is clear about this. "It's all right to have a beautiful face; it's all right to have *anything*, as long as you don't let these things bring you anxiety and fear. If they come to you, let them come; enjoy their presence. But when they go enjoy their departure too." Who knows, he says, what their leaving might be making space for?

When the idea of something changing causes so much fear that you become fixed, that is *avidya*. The solution is discernment, the ability to tell the difference between permanent and temporary things. If only that were easy.

Transforming

Prior to my transition, I was constantly agitated about how people perceived me. For most of my adult life, that agitation manifested as concern about whether I was being seen as female enough.

Femaleness felt like an ongoing performance that I never got any better at, no matter how long I kept at it. I can only speak from my own experience, but for me, being trans felt like I was wearing an enormous, heavy, full-body costume, complete with mask.

In my own mind, it was utterly obvious that the costume wasn't me. But whenever I tried to say, "This isn't me!" I was told that I was crazy, or that I was making people uncomfortable, or that "everyone wears masks." It felt impossible to convey the depth of the gulf between the costume and my true self or the exhaustion of carrying it. Eventually, I began to believe what everyone else seemed so sure of, that the costume *was* me, after all.

I leaned into the performance of femaleness, despite still feeling like a ham actor flubbing my lines. Every day I thought, *they must see how badly I'm doing this.* One of the strangest experiences of being trans was how few people ever did.

No amount of acting made the discomfort go away, and over time, the fatigue and exhaustion became overwhelming. Coming out as trans, and then deciding to pursue transition, let me finally remove the sweaty, clumsy costume I'd been wearing my whole life. I felt the sun on my skin for the first time in decades. It was like being suddenly a hundred pounds lighter. Whereas before, it felt vitally important to monitor and examine every single reaction ("*Did they see my secret? Were they convinced by the costume?*"), now I could relearn how to speak and act from my own self.

Transition was also a hard lesson in accepting that not everything can be changed. Testosterone has reshaped my physical body and deepened my voice, but it can't make me six feet tall or narrow my hips. Top surgery utterly transformed my life and my sense of self, allowing me to literally stand up tall and to reclaim my confidence in the world because I wasn't expending all my energy trying to separate myself from my own body. A part that had always felt like a stapled-on fake appendage was gone, and it was amazing. But my chest will never look like I was born this way.

My scars will always give me away to those who are watching for such things. This is the other side of the temporary world, or *prakriti*: it may change when we don't want it to, but it may also refuse to change in the ways we desire.

Discernment in my own journey came to me as I began to understand the difference between avoidable distress in my physical and emotional selves and the existential suffering that comes from entangling my Self with those things. Top surgery, testosterone, wearing clothes that make me feel comfortable and alive, and identifying as trans are all forms of "removing the thorn from my foot." They also help ensure that I won't "step on the thorn again in the future" because once I told the truth about myself to the world, I didn't feel the same pressure to get back into the costume to make other people comfortable.

There are now people in my life who have only ever known me as Mark. When they look at me, I don't feel them searching for the double image of who I was before, and I don't feel like I'm playing two parts. The emotional and existential burden of hiding has been lifted.

Avoiding the suffering that can be avoided, including seeking medical care to address physical discomfort and therapy to work through emotional distress, are not only allowed but necessary. It's part of working from the outside in, clearing the brush, allowing yourself to become ready to address the spiritual work that needs to be done. In many cases, my own included, it's not even possible to see what inner work is necessary until the outer brush is cleared.

Many students who take yoga in studios know the word *asana* as a term for the various poses we move through in class. But in Patanjali's yoga, *asana* doesn't mean a series of poses; it means "to attain a comfortable seat" so that spiritual practice can begin. There was no way for me to attain a seat comfortable enough to look inward until I took off the costume and began living in a body that was my own.

And just as Patanjali predicted, the more I removed physical and emotional distress through transitioning, the more I discovered subtler forms of impermanence beneath the surface. When I first came out, I wanted to "fix" myself as male, but the more my body felt like my own, the more I understood that being fixed at the male end of the spectrum was just as bad a fit for me, and just as exhausting, as being fixed in femaleness. That's not true for all trans people. Some find themselves comfortably at one end of the spectrum, others nearer to the middle. I wanted, just as much as anyone else, to have a fixture on which to rest myself and say, *Aha! This is me forever.*

That's not what happened. There are days I feel male and move through the world as male, but even on those days, my history of being female in our culture and in relationships moves with me. On other days, I feel that my body, broad-shouldered and masculine and flat-chested as it is, is a female body. There no longer seems to be a contradiction there. My gender lies beneath.

I have experienced incredible pleasure in my physical transition, including pleasures that cisgender people may take for granted: the pleasure of seeing myself in the mirror, the pleasure of simply going to the grocery store as myself, the pleasure of building relationships in which people can see me. These pleasures are sometimes small, like running my hand across my flat chest and feeling intense gratitude. Occasionally they are revelatory, like being in an intimate relationship in my true body for the first time.

The most powerful of these experiences has been the slow realization that *this is* my true body. There isn't an ideal version out there that would be better, whether that was the unscarred female version from the past or some "real" male version that I would have been, if only. This body is my real one, including all my scars and my complex gender presentation.

Taking the physical needs of my body seriously wasn't a

distraction from some kind of true spirituality that would allow me to hover arrogantly above the world. I've tried that self-denying approach, and I can say from experience that it isn't any form of peace. Discernment, for me, was accepting the complicated relationship between the temporary and the permanent. Whatever my permanent Self is, its gender is complex, fluid, multifaceted, and somewhere in the middle of male and female. Allowing my body to more and more closely reflect that fluidity allowed me to see both myself (my physical and temporary being) and my Self (the underlying, eternal part) more clearly.

So now, as I read the *Sutras* again, I more often read impermanence as fluidity.

Fluidity is what allows us the space to flow around and through the multitude of our potential Selves to discover where we truly live. As my testosterone levels rise and fall, I see the impermanence in various aspects of my new body. As my sense of gender shifts even from one day to the next, I let go of the need to be, or to be seen as, one thing or another. This discovery of fluidity has been a doorway into understanding what the *Sutras* mean by *prakriti*, the temporary world.

Fluidity recognizes the seasonality and cyclicality of *prakriti*. To call the temporary world "impermanent" creates the impression of a one-way movement in time. It suggests death. Everything ends, nothing lasts, the world falls apart and decays. All of these things are true, but they are only half the truth, and I think this half-truth is responsible for the belief that yoga is a world-rejecting philosophy. If everything is changing, it can also change toward pleasure, and more importantly, toward joy. Even change is only temporarily moving in any particular direction.

Fluidity is also the precondition for growth. It is the practice of unfixing ourselves. Transness is a very visible experience of fluidity, but the lessons apply to everything that lives on earth. Fluidity is play. It's creativity. It asks us to consider, "What if this thing I am experiencing isn't part of my Self, but an element of the temporary world that I can interact with, love, and hold, even though eventually it will be set aside?"

About two years after my divorce, I went through a period of intense grief. Those of you who have experienced grief will understand this, that grief itself is fluid. I have been blindsided by it on some of the happiest days of my life and felt none for weeks afterward. During this particular period of grief, I had a dream. In the dream, I was going through my old house with my husband, separating our things. The process was as painful in the dream as it had been in life. As I was going through our shared possessions, I looked up at him and said, "You know, I still love you. The feeling is still there. But that feeling isn't enough."

I woke up heartbroken all over again, but also amazed at my mind's ability to know intuitively what I hadn't quite figured out consciously. Love is, in my opinion, part of the eternal Self, maybe the defining characteristic of it. But the forms, the objects, the shapes, the relationships that arise from that love are fluid. They shift and realign. I can feel my loving Self pull back from the world when I hurt and reaching out when I experience joy, but it's always there. That will never change.

Fluidity is the acknowledgement not only that we live in a temporary world, but that we love it. We don't want to lose it. That's not a bug in the system to be fixed. Our love of temporary things is a series of reflections of the eternal love that runs unchanging beneath. We learn from them how to see and access and ultimately rely on the steady current below the waves.

Sri Satchidananda asks us, "Who is the one who loses?" and "Who is the one who hurts?" I am now asking myself, "Who is the one who loves?" In this way, I am seeking what does not change.

Impermanence is a characteristic of the world, but fluidity is a practice: the practice of *finding our own balance* between the permanent and the impermanent, and allowing ourselves to move back and forth from fixed to unfixed and back again. Fluidity and impermanence are the reasons we can start on quests in the first place. Where we are is not where we have to stay.

There is no correct answer to what the quest should look like. To say that this way or that way is the correct way of living in the world is the very epitome of fixation. Each person's balance is different. That's why self-awareness, self-study, and turning our attention inward are so important in yoga. These practices form the basis of all our knowledge.

**Impermanence is a characteristic;
fluidity is the practice. Even impermanence is fluid,
with tides of being fixed and unfixed,
tides of grief and struggle, tides of joy.
I address the pain that can be alleviated
and invite the pleasures that enrich my life.
And meanwhile I ask, "Beneath the changing tides,
where am I? What must become unfixed for me to
continue my quest?"**

Chapter 5
Knowing

WHEN I FIRST UNDERSTOOD THAT I MIGHT BE TRANS, I DID what every modern spiritual seeker does when they need information: I went on Reddit.

To be fair, I got information on Reddit that I could never have gotten anywhere else, since I didn't know any trans people at the time. I read first-hand accounts of top surgery (good and not-so-good), explanations about the effects of hormones, and links to advocacy resources and scientific studies. What I saw most of all, though, was other people like myself pouring out their uncertainties to the community.

Am I trans? How did you figure out that you were trans? How can you tell if you're sure about being trans? What are the signs that you are definitely trans? Can you be 100% sure you are trans? How will I be sure I'm ready for top surgery? How did you make the decision to get hormones?

I've seen news stories that claim trans people are getting hormone treatments and gender reassignment surgeries "at the drop of a hat," but in my experience, the road to transition is a long one, punctuated with periods of doubt and periods of momentum.

I've watched friends go back and forth on the transition teeter-totter for months. *Should I, shouldn't I?* It is, after all, a complex decision with potentially life-altering effects.

No wonder we ask ourselves, in so many different ways, "How can I *know?*"

It's not a question that's unique to trans folks or gender transitions. I've asked it myself many times, when I've considered changing jobs or going back to school or starting or ending relationships or moving to a new city. Every time we make major decisions in our lives, we come back to this same central problem. How can we *know?*

The study of what counts as valid knowledge is called epistemology, and it's a major component of almost every philosophical, spiritual, and religious system in the world, as well as every major scientific and academic field. The epistemology of any system tells us what that system considers to be acceptable evidence for truth or a valid basis for making a decision. In chemistry, for example, truth must be demonstrated by experiment or by mathematical proof. Many religions consider faith itself to be the basis of truth: the stronger the feeling of belief, the more true it must be.

If we are to practice yoga—if we're going to dedicate ourselves wholeheartedly to it—we need to know what the *Sutras* consider to be truth. Otherwise, how will we know whether we are on the right path? How will we choose that practice or this one or decide to commit to one studio or teacher or method over another? Patanjali addresses this question in the *Sutras* at great length. He first outlines the problem of ignorance, or *avidya*, which we discussed in the last chapter, then sets out to solve it by providing us with methods to understand what is real and what is not.

In fact, the *Sutras* offer two answers to the question "how do we know?" The first tells us how to recognize the truth of the everyday world we live in. The second goes deeper and tells us how to know *who we really are.* The questions could be phrased:

"How do I know what to believe about the world?" and "How do I know my true Self?"

Radical Knowledge

I studied epistemology in graduate school, and when I talked about it, people would roll their eyes. "Oh, my god," they would moan. "Not again. Why do you care about this so much? It's so *boring*."

The question of what counts as valid knowledge is not a merely academic inquiry. It may sound dry, but this same question has been at the heart of every major revolutionary movement in human history. Even the American Revolution revolved around whether the People know what's best for them, or whether that knowledge belongs to an aristocracy.

Think of Galileo, brought before the Catholic church in 1633 to defend himself against a charge of heresy. The story goes that he called upon the church to validate his findings by looking through his telescope. Rather than take up the challenge, the inquisitors simply refused to look. A telescope was not a valid way of knowing the world, and the Bible was, and therefore there was no need to even check.

Bryant, whose commentary focuses on the place of the *Sutras* in the broader traditions of Indian religious and spiritual life, says that "One can read the entire religious and philosophical history of post-Vedic India as a rejection of Vedic ritualism." Some of the post-Vedic texts, he says, included "a sometimes quite scathing criticism of the ritualistic mind-set." The ritualism Patanjali and others were critiquing was the system in which priests of a particular caste were seen as the conduits between individuals and God. The way everyday people interacted with religion was to perform rituals and to give offerings to the priests. Not all that different from the Catholic church in Galileo's time.

Patanjali takes up the question of what counts as valid knowledge, in other words, as a question of personal liberation—not political liberation, as in the American Revolution, but spiritual liberation. He is asking, "What counts as a valid spiritual experience?" Do you get to choose the direction of your own quest? Or do you have to follow the path dictated to you by tradition and ritual?

The 20th century spiritual teacher Ram Dass, in one of his most popular lectures, says that spiritual inquiry starts with saying, "I want to know who I really am." Patanjali is saying, "*Only* I can know who I really am." Every person can remove their own suffering and access the joy of connecting with the divine Self through their own, individual self-realization.

That was radical 3,000 years ago, and it's still radical today. That radical departure from ritualism is the context in which we have to understand Patanjali's system of "right knowing."

Right knowing comes from three sources, Sri Saraswati explains: "sense evidence, inference, and testimony." Sense evidence is direct perception. It means to see or experience something for yourself. No ritualism required there.

Inference, the second form of right knowing, is the ability to use logic. When we see smoke, it is logical, and therefore valid, to infer fire. To be valid, though, such inferences must be based on clear, necessary connections between two things (such as smoke and fire). We have to have experienced the connection between them firsthand before we accept the inference.

The third form of valid knowledge is testimony or reliable authority. Most translations equate reliable authority with the scriptures, although it's important to note that they don't just mean the *Sutras*. The yoga tradition has always embraced other faiths as paths to the same destination, especially since yoga itself is a practice, rather than a specific faith or religion. Wherever it arises, though, testimony is only valid when it comes from someone who has direct experience or perception of the thing in question. A statement should not automatically be accepted as the truth because a person who calls themself holy has said it. You still have to find out for yourself.

Personal, individual, direct experience of reality is not only the highest form of valid knowing in the *Sutras*; it is the basis of all the others. Inference is only valid when we have personal experience of the relationship between two things. Authority should only be believed when the person speaking has had direct, personal experience of what they are teaching.

Bryant calls this the "hierarchy of Yoga epistemology." When it is available, direct perception is always the highest form of right knowing. He cites one ancient authority as saying that although through scripture or inference a person can learn the basic truths of yoga, "such theoretical knowledge" does not prevent suffering or "give one direct perception of the soul. Therefore, in an immediate sort of way, one is hardly better off than an ignorant person who does not know these things."

A person who has read and followed the scripture word for word is *hardly better than an ignorant person* who has never heard of them? Those are nearly fighting words in the context of ritualism. The right to know yourself is radical in any age, which is why scripture is so often used to keep people from doing it.

Patanjali is making a powerful argument for the ability—and the *right*—of every individual to perceive, interpret, and act on their own personal experience of the world. In this sense, right knowing isn't a debate about accurate knowledge, per se. It's a call to each of us to be responsible for what we believe and how we act. We must have the courage to go beyond the scriptures and rituals handed down to us and make direct contact with our own souls. It's not just that we are allowed to stand up and pursue our own quest for self-realization. He's telling us that, ultimately, that's the only way we'll get there.

It's a bold call to personal ownership, and not an easy one to take up. In part, it's not easy to take up because of the problem of discernment. The *Sutras* go to some length to point out that our senses aren't necessarily reliable. So what do I do when my eyes or ears deceive me? How can I trust what I perceive? How can I make a choice about the future, given that direct perception of it is not yet available to me? How can I know what is the valid, underlying truth versus what I simply "directly perceive" with my confused and impermanent senses?

As always in the *Sutras*, the answer is to get a little closer to the truth, one direct perception at a time. Or in Satchidananda's terms, to try to be a little less wrong.

A Better Ignorance

In the interest of understanding, let me share with you an example of my own ignorance.

There was a time in my life when I believed trans women shouldn't be allowed in women's bathrooms. I am a person raised in a female body who has been sexually assaulted more than once. I heard the arguments that "people with penises shouldn't be allowed in women's spaces" and "women have to be protected," and my fear and anxiety kicked in. Yes, I agreed. Women must be protected! No penises in the women's room!

In that way, I let my fears override my heart. Needless to say, this was long before I realized I was trans myself. At the time, I didn't know (or didn't realize I knew) any trans people at all. Theoretically, I was a supporter of trans rights. But what a difference personal experience makes.

To be clear, none of the people who assaulted me was trans. Not one of them was a cisgender man who dressed up in women's clothes to enter a bathroom. None of the assaults took place in bathrooms or changing rooms, although one did occur in a doctor's office, as part of an exam designed to "prove" that I was lying about being assaulted.

That exam, by the way, was specifically created to come between my direct experience of what happened and my parents' desire to pretend it didn't. It enabled my father to say, "I'm not convinced." He couldn't look me in the face and say it. He said it to the psychiatrist who read him the report that she didn't write, based on the exam that none of them saw and that, by the way, was performed in a way not according to any known research or validation. Direct experience is powerful; that's why we as a society often go so far out of our way to avoid it. Ritualism is not dead. It merely takes new forms.

I fell into it myself when I chose to believe that keeping trans women out of women's bathrooms might be a solvable version of the much more widespread and intractable problem of sexual assault.

The idea that men commonly masquerade as trans women to perpetrate assaults in bathrooms is what Patanjali calls *vikalpa*, or delusion. Delusion occurs when we form opinions about things that don't exist in reality. The people who created and spread the notion of trans women as disguised rapists have had no direct experience of it, because it does not exist.

Patanjali pauses in describing right knowing to spend substantial time laying out the forms of false knowledge, including *vikalpa* —and for good reason. False knowledge can be dangerous, both to others and to our own progress in the practice. He differentiates three kinds of false knowing: *vikalpa* (delusion), *viparyaya* (misconception), and *smrtih* (memory).

Vikalpa and *viparyayah* differ in that *vikalpa* doesn't refer to a real object at all. It's also been translated as "fancy" or "imagination." *Viparyayah*, or misconception, occurs when we do experience a real object, but we believe untrue things about it. Seeing a rope and believing it's a snake falls into this category. Memory, or *smrtih*, is not just ordinary memory, but the inability to let the past go, to let a past experience "escape the mind." False knowledge, in other words, can occur when we experience something but misinterpret it, when we imagine something that isn't there at all but still have strong feelings about, and when we can't let memories go.

As someone with PTSD, I can recognize all of these in my own experience. When I hear a squirrel leap onto my roof but imagine it's a dangerous person entering my home, that's a misconception. Delusion occurs when I imagine that there is a person waiting around the corner to harm me, and it turns out there's no one there at all. And *smrtih*, the kind of memory Patanjali is talking about, occurs all the time. Almost every time I see one of those orange-tinged street lamps, for example, the present world disappears and I am back in a moment of fear that my mind can't let go of.

There is no blame in these descriptions. Patanjali is pointing out to us much the same thing that modern trauma theory explains, that there are mindstates that cause us real, sometimes intense distress that are nonetheless not based in what is actually happening in the present moment. It's not necessary to experience trauma or PTSD to recognize these states, either. The *Sutras* make it clear that everyone is subject to them, simply by the nature of the human mind.

We imagine that others are blaming or criticizing us when they're not even thinking about us. We see that we made a mistake at work and imagine ourselves being fired. We can't let go of that one time we humiliated ourselves in third grade, or the lost love we imagine might have been "the one." Fortunately, Patanjali offers us a method for gently removing these misperceptions.

"For now," Sri Satchidananda writes, "we can get rid of ignorance with ignorance. Take a better ignorance to get rid of a worse one." It's not possible (for most of us, anyway), to push out all our thoughts and misconceptions and stuck memories all at once.

What we can do is "analyze them and eliminate one set after another."

It's as if our misconceptions and delusions are clouding the lamp of our true knowledge, and through our practice, the obscuring darkness becomes thinner and less obstructive, and the light of true knowledge shines brighter and brighter from within.

Sri Satchidananda offers the example of a young person who has spent a lot of time in night clubs but now wants to live a more contemplative life. When a friend invites him to go to the club, he feels "drawn to go," but finally decides, "I have seen hundreds of shows like that; what can I gain by another one?"

Night clubs aren't inherently an obstacle; the obstacle is whatever in your life, at this moment, is keeping you from what you *really* want to do, what will bring you true joy. And that's where *right knowing* comes in. To know what you really want, what really brings you joy, you must have direct experience of the choices and say, "This one brings me the most joy" (or the least suffering).

One of the most famous examples of "better ignorance" is the Buddha. As a young man, he was wealthy and enjoyed all the pleasures of wealth. He set out on his own to find out all the good things in the world, and he enjoyed them. Yet at each turn, he found that eventually, the good things weren't so good anymore. He was not finding lasting joy. So he would turn to something else, first to studiousness and then to asceticism. Every time he had a direct experience of a new way of life, he analyzed himself and said, "What is my own, direct experience of this?" In the end, he found his bliss in stillness beneath a *bodhi* tree.

Even in writing this book, I found myself in the midst of this practice. As long as I was just imagining writing a book, it competed with all the other things I could imagine wanting to do. I also felt blocked by all the misconceptions that swirled around in my head, the fears about whether the book would go well and whether I was capable of writing it or had the right to speak about the subject. It was only by forcing myself to sit down and write that I could directly experience it.

I found that every single time I devoted myself to the task of writing, I felt more in line with my true self. The imaginary draw of all the other things I might be doing faded. The satisfaction I experienced from writing was strong, even when the work itself felt difficult, slow, or badly done. At that point, I decided to clear away some of the other activities I was involved in so that I could focus on this—even activities I truly enjoy and will probably return to when this is done.

When we have to decide what's true, "scripture provides us with information about the path that is to be followed, and inference or logic helps remove doubts about that path," but in the end, we must have "passion" for a "direct *experience* of their truths," according to Bryant. Both Patanjali's scripture itself and books about how to write provided information for me. Inference removed doubt by showing me that other people who had written books were glad they had gone through the process, even when it was hard, which meant that I was likely to have a similar outcome. But only direct experience created the *knowing* inside me that drove my commitment and my behavior.

Thus, right knowledge is the active practice of stepping back and saying, "What is my own, personal, direct experience of this thing? Does it reflect myself as I really am, or is it based on a delusion or a misconception? Does it advance me on my quest toward self-realization, or push me back into fixation or fear?" It may be the human condition to live in ignorance to one extent or another, but to choose the better ignorance in each moment is to be on the road to wisdom, just as clearing away a piece of the brush takes you closer to the light within.

The Light of Wisdom

The word "yoga" is often translated as "yoke," based on the Sanskrit word *yuj*, which can mean to yoke, to join, or to unite. Many Western practitioners will never have seen the type of yoke the word originally referred to: the wooden beam that harnesses animals, usually oxen, together to pull carts or other loads. A yoke holds the animals together and makes them manageable so that they pull in the same direction, under the control of the driver.

But what is the practice of yoga yoking together? Many instructors describe it as a union of "mind, body, and spirit," and there is some truth to that. In the *Bhagavad Gita*, one of the great Indian epics that informs the broader yoga tradition, the god Vishnu, disguised as the chariot driver Krishna, teaches life lessons to the warrior Prince Arjuna on the eve of battle. Krishna uses the chariot as an analogy, saying that our thoughts, our emotions, and our physical sensations are like unruly horses that must be tamed and managed. In that sense, yoga is indeed a practice of yoking together the mind, body, and spirit so that they aren't fighting each other and causing suffering.

But remember that for Patanjali there are two parts to every story: the practice and the goal. The practice of yoga is to still the fluctuations of the mind, those bucking broncos of emotional, physical, and emotional reactivity. Right knowing is part of that practice: through direct experience of what creates mental fluctuations and what calms them, what causes distress and what puts us on the path to equanimity, we understand our own nature more and more accurately. This is the aspect of knowing that relates to the temporary, impermanent world, which includes our constantly-shifting thoughts, emotions, and sensations.

The goal of knowing, though, is to see the truth of the permanent Self underneath all those fluctuations. "Valid or invalid," Sri Satchidananda writes about knowledge, "you will eventually have to set it aside to find your peace." The final state is not knowing at all, but wisdom.

Here we finally understand the point of all our various practices. If the goal is the ultimate aim of self-realization, the practice includes everything that prepares us for and keeps us moving forward on our quest. Clearing away the brush, moving through physical postures to become aware of body and breath, and undertaking the ethical vows to assess whether our actions fit our intentions are all part of that preparation. Every single practice of yoga that gives us direct perception of our own thoughts, emotions, and sensations leads us through these subtler and subtler stages of awareness, to the final stage, which is simply to come face to face with our own Self, as it really is.

In other words, the purpose of yoga isn't to *create* a union between the impermanent self and the eternal Self, but to *recognize* that there was no separation in the first place. This special kind of knowing, this recognition, is called *realization*. Your true Self was always there, the burning light beneath the dirty surface of the lamp.

You can't yoke together what was never separate.

Imagine a star that has pulled so much debris around itself that its light is only visible as reflections off of the bits and pieces that surround it. The star itself cannot be seen, and so we see light reflecting from one of the bits of debris and say, "That is the source of the light." But then that piece of debris flies off into space or falls apart, and we believe the light is gone, until we see it reflected off another piece, closer in to the star and even brighter, and say, "Aha! Here is the true light!"

We are like that star. Our upbringing, our experiences, everything that happens as a result of our living as embodied creatures in the world make up the debris. Just as the star holds the pieces to itself with gravity, we hold onto appearances and memories, not wanting to let go of what appear to be aspects of our own self. But with each one we let go, we see the reflection of the true inner Self a little brighter, a little closer in.

Each newly revealed, slightly brighter reflection seems to be the true Self. I have been through this cycle time and time again. I change jobs, and the new job aligns better, and I think, *Aha! This is the true Self!* But of course, that feeling does not last forever. I study psychological concepts about the self, like personality types or parts work, and I say again, *These ideas reveals my true Self to me at last!* But no.

I marry the love of my life, or so I believe, and say, *This is forever.* I recognize that I'm trans and think, *I've finally arrived.*

When you are in this process, remember that the grief you feel at each disillusionment may be temporary, but it is real. Give yourself compassion. Uncovering the true Self is not a process that can be hurried, and peeling off layers that you believe to be parts of your own being is almost always painful.

Eventually, though, all the pieces are cleared away, and we realize that the star was the true Self all along. After that, new pieces can come and go, but we won't be fooled by their reflections. The star was always part of the eternal universe, always in the right place in the night sky. It was never the bits of debris. Therefore it doesn't need to be yoked to anything, just uncovered.

As Sri Saraswati explains, "yoga is union, but it must be remembered that it is disunion first." We have to put down and let go of all the bits and pieces. Only then will we realize the underlying truth, that we were never separate from our true Selves in the first place. The entire practice of yoga exists in the space between how apparently simple this idea is and how incredibly difficult it is to achieve.

Fortunately for all of us temporary beings, yoga is compassionate. The Self is always there waiting for you, no matter how long you take. And there is even better news: every single act of practice, every layer peeled away, every step inward on the journey, brings us closer to the warming light of true wisdom.

Transforming

In the middle of trying to decide whether and in what ways to pursue gender transition, I found myself at an impasse. I'd read the scientific literature and studied every individual story about transition I could find, whether on the internet, in books, or from people I knew in person. In a sense, these acted as scripture and inference. The scientific literature showed me the path that could be taken, and the human stories gave me faith that, if so many others had pursued transition and found happiness, perhaps I could, too.

I finally reached the point where there was no new information to be gathered. Every story I read was a repeat of a story I'd read before. Every new study I found (few as they were) laid out the same pros and cons and the same basic evidence.

I found myself asking the question that we all have to face at one time or another: how do I develop the courage to stop relying on authorities, or on the voice of the community, and act for myself? Until I did that, I could not really know whether transition was for me. Only my own, direct perception of its specific effects on my body and mind and heart could tell me that.

That was when I first heard the term "gender euphoria."

When we talk about transgender people in America, we often talk about the concept of gender dysphoria, which is the experience of a disconnect between a person's felt sense of their own gender and the sex they were assigned at birth. Many (but not all) trans people experience gender dysphoria. Some people who are not trans experience it, too.

Gender euphoria is the inverse. It's the feeling of being aligned with the gender you feel inside. A lot of trans people experience gender euphoria for the first time when we start to transition, and it's a novel and sometimes overwhelming feeling. Gender euphoria can come from hearing your chosen name addressed to you for the first time, or shopping in the part of the store that fits your sense of your true self, or starting hormones, or coming out to a loved one.

My first experience of gender euphoria happened on a Zoom call, in a meeting with my work supervisor. I'd only recently come out to myself as trans, and I was nervous about telling her the news, especially since I didn't know how clients would feel about my transition or whether the company would support me.

Being a direct person, and wanting to get it over with, I barely waited for her to say hello before blurting out, "I think I'm trans!"

I was not at all prepared for how she reacted. In the best case scenario, I had imagined her being tolerant, maybe even accepting. She was *thrilled*.

"Oh, that is so exciting! Thank you for telling me!" She was smiling so hard, I was almost afraid I'd told her some other news. I could feel myself smiling back. I had never imagined someone could be this happy for me, just for discovering a piece of myself.

Even so, I thought that would be it. Surely we would move on to the agenda for the meeting now. But she surprised me again. "Do you have a name you like to be called?"

My heart almost stopped. I hadn't shared my new name with anyone except my intimate partner and my therapist, and with them it was still a "what if." I'd never heard it said out loud to me as if it was really my name. I remember sweating and blushing, stammering so hard I could barely get the words out. "Some people . . . I mean . . . . I prefer the name Mark," I finally managed.

"Okay, Mark!" She smiled some more and then started laughing. "You should see your face," she said. "You're *beaming*."

And I was beaming. The sides of my mouth were stretched so hard they were sore. I tried to rein it in, but I couldn't. *She called me Mark.* That was all I could think. Everything else was wiped from my brain. *She called me Mark. I am Mark. That's who I am.*

At moments like these, I lament the limitations of the English language. How can I express the feeling of showing my true self to someone and having it not rejected but celebrated? How can I describe the first moment in my life when I was allowed a direct experience of Mark's existence in the world outside my head? How can I tell you the fear that gripped me, or the courage it took to get those words out of my mouth?

In the trans community, there is a saying: "follow the euphoria." It's a rejection of the dominant narrative that, in order to "qualify" as trans, you have to demonstrate overwhelming, even life-threatening dysphoria. For decades, trans people had to essentially perform suicidality in order to access gender affirming care. Transness was only acceptable if it was miserable, dejected, and suffering. We had to be charity cases, supplicating at the altar of medicine and acceptance.

Following the euphoria is a reclaiming of our right to pursue *right knowledge* of our true, authentic selves. It's also a way off of the endless teeter-totter of indecision. Following your euphoria is a *practice* of making one choice at a time, no matter how small, and seeing how it feels. Ask a friend to call you by your chosen name. If that creates joy for you, ask more people to use that name. Set an appointment to talk with a doctor about gender affirming care and notice how you feel when you see it on your calendar.

The practice of following the euphoria is a form of the practice of right knowing: moving toward the deeper truth about yourself one direct perception at a time.

And it's not always a one-way street. Peeling off the layers that surround the true self sometimes reveals a layer below that we did not expect. Exactly where an individual trans person—or any person—will end up as a result of this practice can't possibly be known ahead of time. That's what's so terrifying about it, and it's why we want to rely on the scriptures and the accepted community voices instead of treading dangerously out into the waters of direct experience. But in no other way can we gain right knowledge. And without right knowledge, we have nothing to guide us forward in the quest for reunion with the Self.

Recognizing my own gender euphoria was a pivotal moment in my trans journey, and it turned out to be pivotal in my yoga practice as well. It was the moment I understood that yoga is not just a practice for moving away from suffering. It is also, maybe even more so, a practice of moving toward joy. In the same way that pain and distress offer us information about the true sources of our suffering, pleasure and happiness can point us toward deeper, more lasting joy.

Gender euphoria also helped me see the importance of the two different meanings of the word "realize." The *Sutra* commentators often refer to realization as the moment of gaining true inward knowledge of the Self. But *to realize* also means "to make real," to bring something into reality, or to cause it to happen. We realize a plan when we put it in action. I realized my trans identity inwardly first, but then I brought it into shared experience so that others could see and interact with it. Transition is itself an ongoing process of realizing: coming to understand a new layer of the self and then bringing it out into the world.

How much a person's gender transition can be realized in the external sense depends very much on their circumstances and on the political, cultural, and familial climate they find themselves in. Inner realizing is available to everyone, but realizing in the context of community is often available only provisionally or in part.

These two kinds of realization are key for all of us, not just for trans people. To realize internally without the ability to make real puts us in a constant state of tension between ourselves and the world, or leaves us in doubt forever because we cannot experience the direct perception of a realized Self that would give us accurate knowledge about it.

And thus we come to the central question the *Sutras* pose to all of us. If the practice is as (apparently) simple as using the knowledge of our own experience to move away from suffering and toward joy, why don't we do it?

To take even one step toward knowledge of the Self, leaving behind the scripture we've been handed and the voices of those who would define us, is an act of radical courage.
Every day, I wonder, "How can I find a better ignorance? How can I uncover even one tiny sliver of my own star, and what might realizing its light in the world do for myself and others?"

Chapter 6
Attachment

THERE'S A FAMOUS VIDEO OF THE CLIMBER CHRIS SHARMA, who won his first World Nationals at 14 years old, completing a roped route at a competition. What's amazing about the video isn't that he climbs well or that he's strong. Of course he does, and of course he is. What's incredible is that he stops about two-thirds of the way up the route for what feels like *eons*. He leans nonchalantly backward at an impossible-looking angle from the underhung wall, lazily shaking out one arm and then the other. Every time you think he's going to start climbing again, he switches hands and shakes out some more.

He looks like he's standing on a subway platform, waiting for the train, not hanging horizontally, forty or fifty feet up, attached only by a metal clip. His grip on the holds is loose and open-handed. It's clear that his muscles are tired, or he wouldn't have stopped to shake them out. But instead of ratcheting up his exertion and pushing upward as fast as possible, he slows down and releases.

As a rock climber myself, I love introducing new people to climbing. The more beginners I bring with me, the more I see that the difference between a so-called expert climber and a novice isn't so much strength or technique, although those matter. The biggest difference is what happens when they get exhausted or scared.

Climbing is hard. It involves heights and danger and putting your life literally in the hands of the person holding the other end of the rope. It uses muscles and movements most people don't use in their daily lives. Exhaustion and fear are inevitable. When a new climber gets tired or scared, they cling on as tightly as they can. Often, they're grasping the holds so tightly that I can see the white-knuckled strain from the ground. The more afraid they are, and the more fatigued they feel, the harder they grip. There's even a term for it. It's called *overgripping*.

Paradoxically, the best thing to do when you're scared and exhausted on the climbing wall is to loosen your grasp. Not let go, necessarily (although trusting the rope to hold you is part of the process, too), but simply relax your hands. Maybe lean into the wall for support instead of relying on your fast-fatiguing arm muscles to hold you.

Attachment is the yoga term for overgripping, for our habit of clinging so tightly to particular ways of seeing ourselves that, instead of security, we find increasing fear and fatigue.

The Gray Nothing

Attachment is often taught and understood through its opposite: nonattachment. Nonattachment, or *vairagya*, is one of Patanjali's two keys to yoga, along with *abhyasa* (committed practice). Unfortunately, nonattachment is often taught in a way that makes people wonder, "Why in the world would I want that?"

In my very first yoga teacher training class, our teacher explained nonattachment to us by saying, "When you achieve nonattachment, everything is the same. There's no suffering.

Nothing makes you particularly happy or particularly sad. You feel the same no matter what happens." A later teacher from another yoga tradition used almost the same words: "You come to realize that it doesn't matter what happens. Your feelings don't change, no matter what is going on. You react the same way to things that you would previously have called good or bad because you realize that they are all the same."

I'm not ready to accept a form of nonattachment that takes away any concept of good and bad. I think it's utterly inhuman to suggest, as another teacher did, that a truly enlightened person would feel the same about a cancer diagnosis as the birth of a grandchild. My entire body screams, *that cannot be right.* And even if it's right, it's cruel. I believe it is a fundamental human right to *feel*, and I have never believed that Patanjali wanted to take that away.

Nonattachment is in fact supposed to be the highest ideal of Patanjali's yoga. It's the promised state of peace at the end of the rainbow. But the definitions offered by my teachers have felt like literally the end of the rainbow: the end of color and light. Nonattachment as a state of not caring what happens one way or the other, not thinking anything is good or bad, seems like a cop out from the world's real problems and an abandonment of joy and connection.

So what does attachment really mean?

In the *Sutras*, "liking for any object of your choice" is called *raga*, and "dislike for the object" is *dvesha* (also spelled *dwesha*). *Raga* is attachment. *Dvesha* is the other side of the coin: aversion. Just as clinging harder and harder to the object of attachment only fatigues us, pushing the object of aversion farther away never makes it disappear. "When you want to eliminate a habit," Sri Saraswati reminds us, "the more you want to get rid of it, the more powerful it becomes."

We begin to move toward true nonattachment when we

understand that our *ragas* and *dveshas* aren't actually changing the outcome. We can cling and cling as hard as we can, or we can devote all our precious energy to pushing down what we don't want to see, and maybe we get some momentary relief. But the underlying agony is still there. The problems come back again and again.

We are all in this process to some degree. It is incredibly difficult to enjoy positive experiences without wanting them to last forever and grasping onto them as tightly as we can. It's even harder to allow negative feelings to sit in our bodies without wanting to shove them away.

The problem is that, the more we try to maintain our sense of self in these states, the more we have to protect ourselves from contact with reality—until eventually, we find ourselves in a tower, surrounded by a moat, clinging to what makes us most miserable. Fortunately, Patanjali's definition of attachment doesn't have anything to do with giving up emotion or abandoning social justice. Attachment is about *identity*, or identification. To be attached, Patanjali says, is to believe "I am that."

Living in the Tower

Here in the U.S., the Ivy League colleges are considered the very tippy-top of the academic tree. Having one of their names on your resume can open doors and create opportunities. The students who attend are believed to be the best in the nation, and indeed the world. But an article written by a member of an Ivy League admissions committee suggests there's something missing in the Ivy League tradition.

He found that, although highly intelligent and unusually successful for 17- and 18-year olds, the students who attend Ivy League schools don't tend to be innovators. In his experience, these young people were so used to succeeding at everything they did that they became terrified to fail. As a result, they never took any risks.

Of course that's not true of every single person who has ever attended an Ivy League school, but it's a potent example of what attachment really means. We tend to think of attachment to sensory experiences like food or sex, or to physical or status objects like luxury cars and big homes. But what was tripping up the Ivy League students wasn't necessarily attachment to a big-name job or even the promise of a lot of money. It was their identification with smartness and success.

As soon as we say, "I am that," we become attached. We say, "I'm the smart one," and so we avoid anything that might challenge us because it might make us look less smart. We say, "I'm the pretty one" and demand that everyone around us mirror that or else fall into misery. We believe all kinds of "I am that" statements. At a family dinner, the older brother who thinks of himself as the successful one insists on paying for everything, even though he's actually running himself into debt to do it. The woman who believes she is the perfect mother can't acknowledge that her child is struggling, and as a result, she keeps them from getting what they need.

We all know these people, and we all know, secretly in our own hearts, that to one extent or another, we are them. And whether we recognize it or not, it is causing us pain.

Patanjali's word for this kind of pain is *klesha*. It is "a kind of agony which is inside our very being," as Sri Saraswati says. Part of the difficulty of sitting still and meditating is that the "agonies" we've been avoiding in our lives come up all at once. "Everyone feels subconscious pain," Sri Saraswati writes, "but our superficial daily activities do not allow us to be aware of it, otherwise we would see pain in all its vividness."

The highest towers we build for ourselves are the ones tied to the identities we want to maintain, either in our own eyes or in the eyes of the world or significant others. "When we watch a movie or a stage play," Sri Saraswati writes, "we tend to identify ourselves with what is portrayed, and experience corresponding emotions of sorrow, joy, fear, dislike, etc. Although the actors are playing a part, we tend to identify with them and forget that we are mere spectators of what is happening."

When we see parts of ourselves, or some of our roles or behaviors, as good or acceptable, and other parts or roles or behaviors as bad and unacceptable, that is the beginning of attachment and aversion. This is another of the paradoxes of yoga. You would think that the ability to see some of our behaviors as good and others as bad would lead us to positive change, and to some extent, that's true. But identifying with the good behaviors or desires and denying the bad ones leads us not toward positive change, but toward clinging.

Attachment happens when I see one part of myself as so good or worthy or laudable that I cannot stand to see any part of myself, or any of my own behavior, that contradicts it. Likewise, if my aversion is so strong that I cannot look at the behaviors or parts of myself that I don't like, I will push my negative feelings away instead of addressing the problem. Honest evaluation of how our behaviors and beliefs serve or hurt ourselves and others is part of right knowing. Clinging to a vision of ourselves that only includes the parts we are proud of pushes us in the other direction.

This is the sense in which Patanjali's concept of attachment overlaps the modern psychological view. In psychological terms, attachment describes how we developed (or didn't develop) safe and supportive relationships with caregivers in childhood. The patterns we develop at that young age often follow us into later life, whether those patterns are secure, anxious, or avoidant.

The anxious pattern is similar to what Patanjali calls attachment: wanting to maintain a positive-feeling relationship with another person so much that you give up yourself or make concessions you don't want to make. The avoidant pattern is similar to aversion, in which fear of being hurt again causes us to build walls or reject connections altogether. Most of us have some blend of these, and they may show up differently at different times.

When we see parts of ourselves we don't like, or have experiences that make us feel bad, we run from them—again, by any means necessary. Unfortunately, this often causes us to externalize the bad feeling onto other people around us, or to try to control their actions. When my mother gets a momentary glimpse that she might have done something she doesn't feel good about, she shoves the feeling away with "jokes" that land the bad feeling on someone else: "If you're mad at me, I'll hit you." Abusive people are often strongly in the grip of aversion, unable to accept the dirty reflection they see and needing to offload their negative feelings onto others.

Of course, that doesn't work. The negative feelings, the aversions, are still there. So the cycle escalates and the person is increasingly committed to doing whatever it takes to maintain the positive feelings and get rid of the negative ones.

It can seem as if we would always be attached to positive self-images and have aversion to negative ones, but that's not always the case. I have a friend who has always perceived themself as likeable and instantly accepted in any group. In their trans journey, this shows up as an aversion to presenting as their true self or changing their appearance, no matter how much they inwardly want to. Every time they make even a slight change toward what they really want, they experience emotional turmoil and stress. They have an aversion to self-expression.

I, on the other hand, was raised as the scapegoat in my family, which required me to see myself as "the problem," the bad one, and so on. For years, anything that contradicted that belief had the power to make me uncomfortable. I was attached to feeling like a bad person.

Neither of these is better or worse than the other. Patanjali doesn't describe *kleshas* and attachment because he wants us to feel bad about how we've responded to the conditions of our lives. He wants to show us the source of our agony.

It's also important to remember that in many cases, we have developed our attachments and aversions as bids for survival. To try to simply pretend they aren't there, or push them down or ignore them, is another form of attachment or aversion in itself. Yoga is always, always a practice and a process.

That said, just as our coping mechanisms may have helped us survive but now cause us pain, living in the locked towers of attachment and aversion will not actually keep the agony out. A force field requires a massive generator. A tower must be constantly built up and maintained. Attachment and aversion require so much emotional energy that letting them go, no matter how terrifying or slow the process, creates incredible space for true enjoyment of our lives.

That is what Patanjali is showing us: first, that the tower exists, and second, that it is not serving us the way we think it is. As long as we keep living there, all we can do is brick ourselves in deeper. We suffer more in the tower than we would from experiencing any feeling, however hard to accept.

And, And, And

My therapist has a brass ampersand on the table in her office to remind us that more than one thing can be true. This *and* that. It's a small but powerful symbol of an expanded way of seeing ourselves. If Patanjali's list of all the "or" options invites us into all the various forms of practice, embracing "and" is the beginning of nonattachment. What happens when we open our grip?

In order to know who we really are, to obtain right knowledge of our Selves, we have to gain direct experience. That's not possible as long as we are living in the Tower. We have to open ourselves up to new experiences and, even more importantly, to new ways of seeing ourselves. Perhaps I'm not who I thought I was. Perhaps I'm something else. Maybe I'm even something additional, something *more*.

Leaning into that kind of openness can be as terrifying as getting 50 feet up a rock wall and looking down. You're suddenly desperately aware of the nothingness below you. Your brain starts to calculate what it would feel like to hit the ground.

One of my friends was mostly paralyzed by a fall from a rock wall, inside a climbing gym. I know how dangerous it is. I understand anyone who doesn't want to do it.

But knowing who we really are isn't that kind of choice. If you never go rock climbing in your life, you might be missing out on something fun, but that's all. If you stay walled up in your tower of self-identifications and never venture out to find your true Self, on the other hand, you are prolonging a suffering that could be alleviated. The *Sutras* hold that you'll come back again and again, in one life after another, until this lesson is learned, so you might as well start now. Even if you don't believe in literal reincarnation, though, retreating into the tower to avoid learning that you are more, and different, than the parts of yourself you identify with is still a source of suffering.

The starting point to loosen our grip on our identifications is "and."

I am a socially anxious person and an introvert, and I want to get out into the world and meet people and live expansively.

My primary purpose, as I see it, is to seek union with my divine Self, and my physical self lives in the world and desires safety, comfort, and companionship.

I am a scholar, and an athlete, and a devotee.

I have experienced terrible trauma in my life and will always, in some way, be healing from it, and I have always been whole.

I am person who seeks a retreat from the world, and a person who runs toward it with curiosity and love.

I am a person with all the limitations of humanity, and I am a limitless spiritual being, always already at one with the divine Self.

The wall—the force field—that I put up was designed to protect me from a dangerous world, and it was always also standing between me and my expanded self.

A tree has buds, and green leaves, and brown, brittle, dry leaves, and no leaves at all. None of these is the "real" form of the tree. Or rather, all of them are the real form of the tree. Likewise, we are many things, *and* they are all real fruits of the Self, *and* all the while the true Self remains the same.

Part of my own practice recently has been to intentionally embrace the "and." To open up rather than close down. On a recent morning, for example, I was experiencing a lot of what I call my "jangly" feeling. It's a feeling I associate with PTSD, and it causes me to be extra sensitive to everything. Usually, when I feel jangly, I cocoon myself in my big headphones, close all the doors and windows, and hope it passes. I close myself in my tower and then proceed to feel trapped, and angry with the world for trapping me.

On this particular morning, I decided to do something new. I opened all my windows and propped open my front door. It let the sound in, yes, but also the breeze, and the dancing shadows of the trees. For the first time, I felt like part of the neighborhood and its life instead of the holder of an embattled fortress.

My jangliness did not magically disappear. I wasn't "cured." I don't leave my door open (physically or metaphorically) all the time, or to everyone. But moments like these have brought me closer to understanding Patanjali's lesson about attachment, that trying to protect myself from life, from parts of myself I don't want to look at or feelings I don't want to have, can become a form of imprisonment. To escape our prison, we must open ourselves to new ways of being. Often, the first step toward opening up is falling apart.

Transforming

In Tarot, the Tower card is one that most people dread seeing. You might think that the Tower card would signify towering success, or a pillar of strength, but in the traditional decks, the Tower represents disintegration. It's almost always depicted as a Medieval-style stone tower being hit by lightning and literally falling to pieces. The people who were safe inside are thrown to the ground to start building all over again.

Needless to say, the Tower is not as popular as the cards that signify imminent prosperity or new relationships.

But the Tower is a powerful card, one of the so-called Major Arcana. It signifies falling apart, yes, but also the opportunity to build back up. Once thrown clear of the tower, the people may be momentarily at a loss, but they are also free to reconstruct their lives any way they want.

When we fall apart, we also—maybe for the first time—get a chance to find out what we're made of. And I mean that in a literal sense. When we go to pieces, we can see the pieces themselves, rather than experiencing ourselves as a single, homogenous unit. In that moment, we see that we're not just one thing. We're many pieces, held together in a particular way by the identity we've created for ourselves, or had created for us. A Lego monster is just a monster, but if you take him apart, you're left with pieces that could become a monster again, or could be transformed into anything you want: a friendlier animal, a boat or airplane for adventuring, or a cozy little cottage to live in. You can pick some pieces to keep and others to lovingly set aside.

Unlike Legos, we aren't just the pieces. We're also the energy that holds those pieces together. Underneath all the various shapes we make out of ourselves is the same underlying Self.

Paradoxically, the key to uncovering the eternal, singular Self is to accept the plurality of the impermanent self in the world. To be plural, or to see ourselves as plural, is to see all the parts that we play, and all that parts that we *could* play, and all the pieces of ourselves that we feel good about and all the ones that we don't like, and to hold them all without identifying with any of them or shoving any of them away. For those who have done parts work (or, more formally, Internal Family Systems), this will feel familiar. It's the idea that there are no inherently bad parts of the self, and no inherently good ones, either.

You can see here how nonattachment is directly related to right knowing. If the Self is like a bright star surrounded by bits and pieces of reflective detritus that we think of as our identity, we won't be able to peel them away and see the star for what it is until we recognize that the detritus is not us. And there is a double meaning of "parts" here: the parts of ourselves *and* the parts we play in the world, including the parts we play on our own internal stage, to show ourselves who we think we are. The two meanings are always intertwined.

Coming out as trans forces this kind of falling apart, this reckoning with the varied and often contradictory parts of the self. As a result, it also pushes us toward the recognition of the consciousness underneath that only seems to be playing different roles. Interestingly, all the *Sutras* commentators mention sex specifically as one of the characteristics that can come or go. For them, being a man or woman was one of the accidents of the temporary world that did not reflect the eternal Self within, which was without gender, or perhaps more accurately, existed before gender.

Transness is a loosening of our grip on our identifications, either as we have defined them, or as we've had them defined for us. Many, many trans people have the experience of over-identifying with the gender they were assigned at birth, in an attempt to be the way they were "supposed" to be, to play the part assigned to them. To recognize transness is to step back from that performance. That often means giving up a great deal, including the validation of the world, relationships with people who want us to continue in the role that they were comfortable with, and sometimes even our livelihood.

But tower moments come to us all. If anything, my divorce crumbled my sense of self more than coming out as trans. I never felt particularly attached to my female identity, whereas my marriage felt, at many times in my life, like the only safe island in a sea of fear. I wasn't just married. My personality and identity were wrapped up in my relationship with that one person. It defined me.

Tower moments can come through the loss of job, the illness or death of a family member, changes in the cultural or political landscape that surrounds us, or a shift in a relationship, even if it's not lost. No tower lasts forever, no matter how much we try to force it to remain in place.

The falling apart of the tower of identity is so terrifying that we can become afraid even when we see it happening to someone else. This is one reason trans people appear threatening, especially if they are genuinely happier and more at peace after transitioning. Seeing someone else change awakens a question that lurks in the backs of many of our minds. *What if there's a part of myself that I'm ignoring? What if I am not happy with my own roles? What if I, too, am playing parts that were assigned to me rather than those that align with my true Self?*

To survive a tower moment, and to avoid simply building the pieces back in the same old comfortable way after it's passed, requires what Patanjali calls *svadhyaya*, or self-study. Sri Saraswati says that in *svadhyaya*, you "perceive your own self in different perspectives." You must undertake "the detailed study of your own self, which includes study of the entire structure of your personality."

For many, many years, I believed that I did not have a soul. Other people might have bright eternal stars inside, but I was empty. I described myself as a shell. A pod person. It was a much, much worse feeling than sadness or grief or pain. I really believed that, perhaps alone in all the world, I had nothing inside. I've since learned that this is a common experience for people who have experienced similar traumas in childhood, but at the time, I simply felt separate and apart from all the rest of humanity.

Seeing and accepting my own plurality was what allowed me to loosen my grip on the detritus just enough to glimpse my own star for the first time. That first glimpse made my decades of practice worthwhile in an instant. Before that, I had been practicing because I knew it was good for me, because it seemed to relieve the burden of my suffering somewhat, because I was told that there was a payoff somewhere in this lifetime or a thousand lifetimes from now. After that moment, I began to practice from sheer joy and gratitude.

I've heard people refer to yoga as "navel-gazing," in part because of this emphasis on self-study. I prefer to call it heart-gazing. What is revealed through *svadhyaya* and nonattachment is the self as it truly is, loving and open and able to withstand even the utter destruction of the tower of identity.

Interestingly, there is an idea in our culture that transness, and gender questioning generally, is also a form of navel gazing, reserved for upper class people who have time to sit around questioning themselves. In fact, trans people often find themselves doing heavy labor, working out the unacknowledged burdens of the broader culture. Which brings us to one of the most misunderstood and disliked concepts in the entire yoga tradition: *karma.*

Whether it falls apart in a single, devastating
lightning strike, or drops to pieces like petals falling
from a tree, I let my tower fall and
survey the pieces with love and curiosity.
What could these pieces become, other than a tower?
Which ones do I choose to keep, even knowing that
they are only parts I'm playing in the world, and
which do I retire with gratitude? How do I design a
practice of self-study that leads me to my own
shining heart?

Chapter 7
Karma

Poor Arjuna.

Perhaps the best known explanation of the concept of *karma* comes from the *Bhagavad Gita*, the early Hindu text that describes Prince Arjuna leading his army into battle. His own army is made up of his kin: members of his family and his close friends. Unfortunately for Arjuna, so is the other army.

As he surveys the battlefield, he sees that in order to win, he will have to kill people he loves. He hesitates, not wanting to give the order to fight, but not wanting to walk away from what he believes is a righteous battle. Fortunately for Arjuna, he has a special guide. His chariot driver, Lord Krishna, turns out to be an incarnation of the god Vishnu, who proceeds to explain Arjuna's situation to him, outlining along the way the basic concepts of Hinduism, including surrender to God and the impermanence of the material world.

As Krishna points out, if Arjuna leads his army into battle, it is true that many of his family and friends will die, but if he chooses not to lead his army into battle, the other side will still attack, and many of his friends and family will die anyway. Whether he fights or does not, the result will be the same. In order to overcome this inner conflict, Arjuna must accept his *dharma*. In this context, *dharma* has two meanings: the duty of an individual person, and the greater social or universal order that rules all things. In order to achieve his own *dharma*, Arjuna must act in accordance with the larger *dharma*, the social order in which he lives and the laws of his religion.

The story of Arjuna still captures, and frustrates, readers today —myself very much included. Arjuna is caught between two bad choices and bound by the rules and expectations of the society in which he lives. These rules have been handed down to him, devised and put in place long before he was born. The seeds of the war he's fighting were also sown years, decades, or centuries earlier. None of what Arjuna is facing was caused by him, and yet he is left paying the cost of these ancient and ongoing tensions with the blood of his family and friends, and with the pain those deaths are causing in his own heart. That cost is *karma*.

Karma has been defined in many different ways and used in many others, often in contexts that seem terrible to me. The caste system in India has been defended on the basis of *karma*, with the idea that people in lower castes must be paying for bad deeds from previous lifetimes. Even in the *Bhagavad Gita*, the implication is that if Arjuna surrenders to God and acts in accordance with the social role he's been assigned, his actions, even killing members of his own family, will be without *karma*.

We often think of *karma* as good or bad. In those terms, it's popular enough that baristas label their tip jars "good karma." In some early belief systems, good karma could indeed be saved up and used to barter with the gods for a better life (or afterlife) or nicer stuff, sort of like indulgences in the early Catholic church.

In most definitions, *karma* is seen as an individual cost: you do the crime, you do the time, so to speak. In that sense, *karma* is essentially the sum total of the consequences of your actions. If you cause harm or behave outside of your duty or act out of selfishness or greed, you rack up bad karma. Traditionally, *karma* is the force that keeps us on the wheel of birth and death, being reborn again and again until we get it right.

The key to that understanding of *karma* is that it sticks to the same person, throughout time if necessary. The person who behaved badly pays the price.

If only that were true. In fact, we only have to look around to see that individuals don't always pay the price for their own actions. Children take on the cost of their parents' bad moods or addictions. Laid-off employees pay for the poor decisions of their CEOs. The traditional concept of *karma* smooths out this unfair distribution of outcomes by saying that each person is called to do their duty in whatever role they've been assigned in this life, and that they probably earned that low position through actions in a previous life. No wonder *karma* isn't a popular concept in the modern world, especially in the West. When I told a friend I was writing this book and said that I was having trouble with the concept of *karma*, she said, "Yeah, you should!"

Poor *karma*.

Like so many of the concepts Patanjali picks up in the *Sutras*, though, his explanation of *karma* is not prescriptive but descriptive. He's telling us, yet again, "Here's where your suffering is coming from." When I step back from my instinctive dislike and my preconceived notions about what *karma* means, I see that Patanjali is merely holding up the mirror again and telling us to look, not at what other people are doing wrong or who is to blame, but at how we are all causing ourselves, *and each other*, pain—and how we can stop.

Before we enter into this chapter, though, I will add that *karma* remains, in my view, massively unfair. The distribution of costs is not, has never been, and probably never will be, equal. We are all caught in the net together, but some are more bound than others. What, then, can we do about it?

The first step is to understand where *karma* comes from. For that, we have to zoom out and take a very wide view of human behavior.

The Cost of History

I wrote my doctoral dissertation on the US Food and Drug Administration (FDA) new drug approval process. In brief, the FDA reviews all the new drugs that are developed by pharmaceutical companies, evaluating them to see whether they work well enough, and are safe enough, to be prescribed. I specifically studied the approval process the FDA went through for a drug called Avastin, a new type of breast cancer drug that had both very high promise and potentially severe side effects. The drug was approved, but then during a later review, the FDA decided to withdraw that approval because of the unclear data about whether it worked, combined with the high risk of side effects.

As part of the process, the FDA held a hearing and invited the drug company, doctors, and patients and their families to speak. The transcript of this hearing is both coldly scientific and heart-breakingly personal. The drug companies and the FDA present evidence in technical, clinical terms, discussing "adverse events" (negative side effects) and "progression free survival" (patients living longer without their cancers growing).

Then, near the end of the hearing, the patients get up to speak. This is the heartbreaking part. Some patients talk about how Avastin has let them live to see a child's next birthday, or to celebrate another anniversary with their spouse. For them, Avastin is a life-saver that must be allowed to stay on the market. But other speakers, the family members and friends of people who have died, talk about the terrible, life-destroying side effects of the drug.

At the end of two high-pressure days, a panel of medical professionals brought in by the FDA have to make a decision. They can remove the drug's approval and take it off the market, or they can affirm its approval and allow doctors to continue prescribing it to breast cancer patients. If they remove the approval, some people with cancer will almost surely die who would have lived if they'd had the drug. If they affirm the approval, some people with cancer will almost surely die of side effects they wouldn't have suffered otherwise. And there's no third option. They have to decide by the end of the two-day hearing.

Sounds familiar, doesn't it? They're in the same dilemma as Arjuna: stuck between two bad options, responsible for the outcome but with no way of knowing what that outcome will be.

In both cases, the cause of the dilemma does not live in the present. Arjuna didn't start the war he's caught up in, and the FDA didn't create the drug (or breast cancer, for that matter). Both are caught in the net of history, their choices narrowed by circumstances they didn't create. And both are constrained and limited by rules that feel unchangeable and inevitable. In Arjuna's case, those rules are social and cultural. He is bound, as Lord Krishna explains, by his role in society and his birth. The members of the FDA panel, as different as they look from Arjuna, are also bound by the social and cultural rules of their historical context. Their role in the hearing is very narrowly defined by regulatory law, tradition, and politics, meaning that, like Arjuna, they have limited options for action.

That limitation and sense of constraint are what make *karma* such an unpopular concept. It's often seen as predestination or fate, a worldview in which we're so bound in the net created by history (our own personal history as well as broader cultural history) that we have no choice and no freedom of action. But as it turns out, that's not quite true. In order to fully understand *karma*, we have to understand the difference between *karma* as a description of the laws of reality, and the separate notion of *karma* as a description of personal action.

The key to understanding this distinction is time.

Karma is the relationship between action and reaction, or action and the results of action. Action exists in the present moment. Right now is the only time in which we can act. Reaction, or the results of actions, can refer to either the past or the future. We are currently experiencing the results of past actions, and we're constantly creating new results that we'll experience in the future.

Karma as action is a neutral term. *Karma* yoga is, in fact, one of the four primary types of yoga designed for the four personalities of humans. *Karma* yoga is the yoga of action, the practice of attaining realization through action in the world. Often, this takes the form of service work, but any action can be undertaken as a practice. The entire premise of *karma* yoga is that we have choice over the actions we take in any given present moment.

We have no such control over the results of actions once they are taken. As Sri Satchidananda says, "When you do *karma*, you reap *karma*." Or in Sri Saraswati's terms, "cause and effect are bound together." The storehouse of past *karma* already exists. We have to live with the results, and there's nothing we can do to change them.

The emphasis on cause and effect has led *karma* to be read as blame. That reading of *karma* comes from the perspective that *karma* exists solely within the individual. But in yogic philosophy, *karma* also refers to the laws of the universe that govern everything, from matter and time to cultural change and personal relationships.

The cultural context in which we live determines how we understand those laws. In the time that the *Bhagavad Gita* was written, they were understood in terms of reincarnation, with the effects of past lives determining the type of birth and life we're experiencing now. Modern psychotherapy might call it intergenerational trauma. But whatever terms we use for it, and however much we may not like it, the tendrils of history do fetter us. From the way our cells are governed by physical laws set in motion eons ago, to the effects of socioeconomic status on our life choices, none of us can avoid the binding force of past actions.

In that sense, *karma* is not blame, but *cost*—and the costs of an action may or may not be borne by the individual who performed it.

Passing the Buck

I once had a corporate job in which I was promoted to be the manager of a team. Part of the team was a group of writers and editors I inherited from another manager. As soon as I started meeting with them, I could see that the team wasn't working. There was constant conflict and blame. Very little could get done without recriminations and tears.

After a lot of one-on-one and team sessions, I figured out that the problem was the team leader. He was angry and critical. He insulted the other members of his team. He used his own personal beliefs as a bludgeon against anyone who disagreed with him. Every interaction with him turned into a fight. In the end, I couldn't let him stay and destroy the work lives of everyone around him. So I met with my boss, the CEO of the company, and we decided that he had to be let go.

Everything was put in order. I met with HR, and we went through all the processes that such a decision requires. Then, on the day we were scheduled to let this person go, my boss—the CEO of the company—simply didn't come in to work. I was a brand-new manager, and it was suddenly my job to hand over the bad news. The person we were firing yelled and threatened us. "I have three kids," he shouted. "What am I supposed to do?" It was one of the hardest moments of my career. I understand why my boss didn't want to deal with it.

I'm not questioning whether we made the right choice. The entire working culture of the team shifted almost immediately. Everyone was happier and more productive. The anger level went nearly to zero. I later found out that the person we fired found another job that was a better fit for him. None of that could have been predicted, but we made a decision and lived with it, and fortunately the outcome was positive.

That doesn't change the fact that my boss definitely passed the *karmic* buck. Starting and growing a company, and wanting the benefits that come with that, necessarily incur the costs of managing people and dealing with the difficulties and downsides of being the decision maker. But he didn't want to pay those costs, and because he had enough power, he could pass them off onto someone else. The fact that the outcome happened to be good didn't change the fact that the emotional and interpersonal costs had to be paid, and that he let someone else pay them.

Passing the buck is how individual *karma* becomes intergenerational, interpersonal, cultural, political, and economic inequality.

Patanjali makes it clear that the *kleshas* of attachment and avoidance are the original causes of *karma*. My boss wanted to maintain his self-identity as the "nice guy." When I confronted him about not showing up, he even said, "I don't like it when people don't like me. I'm not good with the uncomfortable personal stuff." That's attachment and aversion in one neat summary. He was attached to being liked and had an aversion to uncomfortable feelings.

It's depressing to see, up close, how power allows an individual to offload their "unconscious agonies" onto everyone around them, especially when you can simultaneously see it happening, on a large scale, across our entire society and through history. Passing the buck can also rear its head in attempts to "rewrite" what has already happened. The *karma* created in the past cannot be changed. But when people want to avoid the costs incurred by history, they forget that. They start erasing slavery or the Holocaust from history books to avoid paying the emotional and political costs those histories have incurred, or they cut veterans' or retirees' benefits, pretending they can ignore the costs incurred by previous promises. A party system perfectly supports this, as each party pretends that the promises and commitments of previous administrations have nothing to do with them.

Passing the buck also happens at the personal level, in families, and in communities. If I have a dog that barks, but I don't want to pay for daycare or spend the time training it, my neighbors pay the cost of listening to it bark all day. If I can only be in relationships where I am the expert, I can't allow anyone else to express their ideas. If I don't want to confront the parts of myself I'm not comfortable with, I take them out on my family instead.

Often, these costs take the form of labor. A team leader who is constantly angry requires everyone on his team to do the emotional labor of managing his unacknowledged emotions. One of the most invisible costs is what I call existential labor. Existential labor is the work of creating meaning. When someone has an aversion to doing their own existential labor, or an attachment to the existing meaning that they don't want to give up, the result is often that they pass that cost, that labor, onto someone else.

Trans people, for example, take on the existential labor of an entire culture's unacknowledged conflict with gender. Some people are attached to an existing, comforting concept of binary gender because it creates meaning for them. They have an aversion to opening up that concept because they might have to confront questions about their own identities. The existing binary concept saves them the labor of having to ask, "What does it mean *to me* to be a man, a woman, both, neither, or something else?" It's much easier and less costly to fit into what's provided. The existence of a scapegoat is always a sign of *karmic* debt that someone is trying to avoid, often because there is existential labor around their attachments and aversions that they don't want to have to do.

But what *karma* teaches us is that *no cost ever disappears* once it is incurred. Rewriting every single history book in the world will not change what actually happened in the past or the social and cultural realities that are the result of that past. Not showing up to fire someone doesn't make the negative emotions go away. They're just externalized onto someone else.

If that was the end of the lesson of *karma*, it might show us how to move toward acceptance, but it wouldn't offer any solutions to change the situation. That understanding of *karma* would seem, as it has to me in the past and as it has to many others, to require acceptance of a massively unfair and lopsided system of power in which those who benefit and those who pay are rarely the same.

Fortunately, acceptance is not *karma's* final word. Sri Satchidananda relates the past, present, and future versions of *karma* to an archer's arrows. "There are a number of arrows in the quiver," he writes, and at any time, those arrows can be in two different states: "one has already left the bow and is on its way. You have no more say over it. You can neither stop it now nor draw it back." That is the fate of both the past and the future, in which arrows have already been released. But "the second arrow, ready to be aimed, is like the new *karma* you create at each moment. You have full control over it." You can choose not to let it go.

Sri Saraswati uses similar analogies. "The harvest you are reaping cannot be changed, but you can modify the next harvest by changing the seeds and other conditions. The bullet which has been fired cannot be brought back, but the one which has yet to be triggered off can be held up."

If you've ever heard yoga described as attunement to the present moment, this is the crux of that attunement. The present moment is the only one in which we can act, and therefore the only moment in which we can choose not to let loose another *karmic* arrow and continue the cycle of suffering.

The Unloosed Arrow

The *Bhagavad Gita* is often described as a story of fate, even predestination, but in fact, it's a story about *choice*. Arjuna always had a choice. If he didn't, Lord Krishna, the avatar of Vishnu himself, would not have had to show up and instruct Arjuna on how to behave. If Arjuna had no choice, he would simply have acted in whatever way he was predestined to act. He wouldn't have been able to do anything else.

If anything, Arjuna's story shows us how to *stop* acting in ways we can't help. Being in the grip of *karma* means being controlled by history, whether that's our personal history, our family's history, or the broader cultural history. Patanjali refers to the scars of history as *samskaras*. Essentially, *samskaras* are patterns that we keep repeating because they are imprinted in our minds.

Samskaras can occur on the societal level, too. Perhaps a group of people remembers how nice it was to have a particular kind of privilege or how much easier things seemed fifty or one hundred years ago. These "impressions" aren't always accurate, but they create strong feelings of attachment and aversion, which lead to the unconscious repetition of behaviors, and thus, the creation of new *karma*, new costs that must eventually be paid.

The beginning of all *karma*, according to the *Sutras*, occurred so far back in history that no one knows when or how it happened. Nonetheless, as Sri Satchidananda says, "we should try to put an end to it."

Putting an end to *karma* has nothing to do with placing blame or criticizing other people's actions. When humans act according to attachment and aversion, they're simply doing what human beings do. "If a baby dirties his diaper," Sri Satchidananda points out, "you take it out of the crib, clean it, and put on a new diaper. You don't criticize it. If you wish to criticize it, you have no business with that child." So if ending the cycle of *karma* doesn't involve blaming others or criticizing on the one hand, or simply accepting it and acting like the automatons of our unconscious patterns and *samskaras* on the other, what can we do? We can decide not to unloose the next arrow. And beyond that, if we choose, we can take on some of the larger *karmic* debt for the good of others.

Choosing not to unloose the next arrow can happen in even the most seemingly insignificant of human behaviors. Choose not to take that one next drink, or to smoke that cigarette. Choose, this once, to stop yourself before you repeat your parents' pattern of anger on your own child. Take five breaths instead of flipping off the car that cut in front of you. Just as small practices build up into a lifetime of practice, each individual unloosed arrow reduces the overall *karmic* burden of the entire world.

But what about *karmic* debt on a larger scale? What about the costs that we are still paying from the past, and that marginalized groups end up, almost always, paying more than anyone else? Now we are talking about the true meaning of Arjuna's choice.

Once a *karmic* debt exists, it must be paid. Costs don't go away because we don't feel like paying them. I learned that lesson the hard way the first time I got a credit card. Ignoring the collection letters didn't make the debt disappear; it compounded (literally) on itself until I owed far more than the benefits I'd ever received. *Karma* acts the same way. The longer we try to put off paying it, the more we try to externalize it onto others or pass the buck, the more it grows and takes hold. And it doesn't just take hold of us as individuals. It takes hold of entire cultures, until we find ourselves faced off against our own cousins in a war that can't be won without devastating loss.

In those moments, it is possible to choose to pay some of the debt, even though it's not yours. There's a couple who sometimes pick up trash in the park near my house. They're not obtrusive about it. They don't draw attention to themselves. But once in awhile, I'll see them with bags, collecting cans and fast food containers and cast-off fishing line. They didn't make that mess, but they choose to clean it up.

They *choose* to. In our culture, in our families, and in our relationships, one person or group is often paying the debt for another either unconsciously or unwillingly. That does not eliminate *karma*. It creates (justifiable) anger and resentment, and the result is increasing discord—more *karma*, not less.

But when we choose to take on some of the collective *karma* through service, giving up the expectation of a reward and serving only for the sake of others, that *karma* can finally be eliminated. The entire *karmic* burden of the world is made lighter. This doesn't mean giving up your own life or needs. You must, Sri Satchidananda says, have everything you need "to equip you to serve others." Clothes, a home, food, a family, a profession: all of these are part of life, and they can be part of reducing *karma* if "you do everything with the idea that you are preparing yourself to serve others."

It's a high bar and a high calling. It's not for everyone, perhaps, although the *Sutras* suggest that it can be. It's available to all of us if we want it. For most of us, to omit even one repetition of *karma*, to choose not to repeat *samskaras* that cause harm to ourselves or others, is enough.

The entire practice of yoga, from clearing the brush, to recognizing the identities and behaviors that are impermanent rather than part of our true selves, to releasing ourselves as much as possible from attachment and aversion, all lead here. Every practice of self-awareness and self discipline means one less arrow flying around the world, looking for a target, waiting for its debt to be paid. Each unloosed arrow is that much less suffering.

And for those who choose it, there is an opportunity to take on some of the existing *karma* and pay a debt for all of us.

Transforming

In 2024, Chase Strangio was the first openly trans person to argue before the Supreme Court. A lawyer for the ACLU, a transgender man, and a father, Chase was arguing in a case very close to his heart: *United States v Skrmetti*. The case involved Tennessee laws denying gender-affirming healthcare to minors.

He didn't want to take the case. The documentary that was later released about it, *Heightened Scrutiny*, shows in detail the costs that Chase had already paid for being a trans lawyer in the public eye, and his work on *Skrmetti* only escalated the attacks. He was vilified on social media and in public. He feared for his family's safety. And that was all on top of the grueling labor required to prepare for and present oral arguments in front of the highest court in the United States.

Throughout it all, he remained amazingly calm, open-hearted, and focused. He didn't return the arrows slung at him in the media or turn on his opponents with anger. He consistently returned to his love for his community and his desire to serve others.

Chase shows us that Arjuna's story is not a historical relic. Like Arjuna, Chase was faced with an incredibly difficult decision, with no certainty about the outcome. He would have to pay the costs of publicity and vilification whether he won or lost the case. With only the guidance of his own values and commitments, and putting aside his own comfort, he chose what he believed to be his duty. In the *Bhagavad Gita*, Lord Krishna says, "Be steadfast in the performance of your duty, O Arjuna, abandoning attachment to success and failure. Such equanimity is called Yoga." Or as Bryant writes, Arjuna is encouraged to fight "out of a sense of duty rather than out of concern for the outcome that might result for him personally." Chase Strangio is a living example of this highest principle of yoga.

This kind of service is the culmination of right knowing, nonattachment, and practice. In order to choose to serve, you have to know yourself so that you can determine what you believe to be your duty—your role in the ongoing drama. You have to be able to let go of control over the outcome, to relinquish your own attachments and aversions in the name of what you believe is right. And you have to have the practice behind you to be able to find equanimity wherever the bucking bronco throws you.

Most of us will never face a choice quite like this one, or find ourselves so visibly at the center of a historic moment. Most of our quests are less public and more personal. Yet all of us are called to know who we really are, to lay aside, as much as we can, our attachments and aversions, and to choose a quest that ultimately reduces the *karmic* burden on the world.

For me, transition has been an intentional part of this process, not only in terms of coming to know my true self, but as part of my decision to lay down as many of the arrows of intergenerational suffering as I can. I consciously choose not to hand down the assumptions about gender, or about who people are allowed to be, that I was taught. At the same time, my own transition has also given me the strength and courage I needed to be able to serve others.

I saw *Heightened Scrutiny* in the theater, and I spent most of it crying. Partly that was a reaction to the hatred and anger that Chase and other trans people were facing, but partly it was gratitude that someone like him existed in the world, fighting for people like me. His sacrifice is incredibly powerful and inspiring. The most powerful lesson of the film, though, is not captured in the many depictions of Chase sacrificing for his community, but in the final scene. Leaving the Supreme Court building, he and the other lawyers are greeted by a massive, cheering crowd. Chase is called up onto a makeshift platform, and he speaks to the throng of people waiting there—talking not about court battles and lost sleep but about community, resilience, and love.

It is a moment of pure joy.

Why in the world would anyone sacrifice their life for a few court cases they might not win? For that matter, why would yogis bother with all the effort of practice, with the years and years of clearing the brush just to be able to go deeper and do even more? Why give up what we're attached to or open our eyes to the parts of ourselves we don't want to see? Why give up the easy pleasures and the excitement and thrill of the world of *karma*? Why undertake the quest for self-realization at all? Why do all this *work*?

For too many of us, the study of yoga, and the understanding of spiritual practice more generally, stops with the "how." We hear so much about how to be better people, or how to practice, or how to "still your mind" or how to turn your feet in warrior pose, or how to meditate. If we hear anything about the "why," we're told that it's just what we should do, or that we'll feel calmer or that it will be good for the nervous system.

Almost no one would do all this work just for those reasons. They might start. They might make an effort. But the kind of commitment that is required to continue your practice with dedication, with *zeal*, for years or decades or, according to the *Sutras*, for lifetimes, requires a promise worth what you are giving up. To follow the quest to the very end requires a goal worth winning. That goal is the missing piece in what we hear about the *Sutras*, and it is, in my opinion, the most important lesson they have to teach.

The end of all this effort is not calm, or equanimity, or nonattachment. Those are achievements along the way, but they are not the purpose of the quest. The goal, the promise, is joy.

Living in the world, I create debts, and I pay debts.
Where can I choose not to loose just one *karmic* arrow?
Where can I choose to serve the world by voluntarily taking on a debt rather than creating one?
What am I passing on, and what cycle can I stop from repeating itself in my own life, in my family, in my community, or in the world?

Chapter 8
Joy

WE ALL KNOW WHAT SUCCESS WITHOUT JOY LOOKS LIKE.

A mother sees great musical talent in her child and pushes him to perform. Her child's ability, and the praise he receives, becomes a tool to bolster her own ego. As the child grows, he makes music that sounds heavenly, but he comes to hate every moment he sits to practice, and even the applause he receives feels hollow and meaningless. As soon as he can, the child pushes aside his instrument and walks away. The divine music he could have created is lost.

A professor, rather than inviting students in, locks his door at the exact moment class is meant to begin. Any student who arrives even one second late is locked out from learning. The teacher justifies himself with words like respect. His own sense of importance tells him he is right to act as he does. He has achieved the pinnacle of success in his field, but he remains deeply unsatisfied. Students avoid his class. The knowledge he could have shared stays locked inside him.

My parents tell me that since they've "already seen me graduate once," they're not going to bother driving down to attend my doctoral graduation. On the same day, my faculty advisor emails me to say that, since I'm his only student graduating this year, if it's all the same to me, he'll skip it. I put away my gown and don't attend. A goal I've been pursuing for 15 years turns to ash in my heart, and I spend the next decade ashamed to tell anyone I have a PhD.

The mother pushing her child to fulfill her own attachments and the child being pushed—neither of them feels joy in the music being made, no matter how beautiful it is. The teacher who locks his students out to bolster his own sense of importance is defeating his own aim. He gets no joy from teaching, and the students lose the joy of learning. The mother is hurt and angry when the child abandons music. The teacher goes home every night grumbling and irritated with the laziness of his students.

We need joy. It's not a nice add-on to life or what we'll get if we follow all the rules. Joy is an innate experience that tells us who we are meant to be and what direction will bring us fulfillment and peace. Joy creates connection and compassion. Without it, we are rudderless and separate. Joy is necessary.

To fully witness and serve the opening up of human potential requires all the elements we have learned. We have to first clear away the brush that keeps us from seeking a new way of being, whether that means getting therapy to heal our inner wounds or literally cleaning our home so that we can feel calm enough to practice. We have to know ourselves, first to know what needs to be cleared away, what is keeping us, individually, from practicing, and then to understand what form of practice best fits our own self, as we are right now, even knowing that it might change. We have to recognize the impermanence of the things we have identified with so that we can let go of the attachments and aversions that keep us from seeing our true selves and serving one another. We must choose, in each moment, to the best of our ability, to stop releasing *karmic* arrows and incurring more and more debt of unhappiness on ourselves and the world.

It's not easy, or fast, but the outcome is worth all the effort. Sri Satchidananda says, "we need never be afraid of the world if we learn how to enjoy it. We can really enjoy the world and even give all the pleasures to our senses. Nothing needs to be starved. But when? Only when we have found the source and connected part of the mind there—then we can enjoy everything." That connectedness, he says, "is our goal and our birthright—nothing less than that."

The Light of Practice

Being engaged in my practice brings me greater joy than anything else I have ever experienced or undertaken. It's as simple as that.

My life has always been on this path, and it has also very often wandered away from it. Some of my earliest memories I now recognize as moments of union with the divine, the eternal Self. Yet I have also spent days, weeks, months, and even years of my life far from my practice, even denying its existence or value.

The joy of devotion to a spiritual path called to me very early. I felt it in the darkened church with my mother, proving to myself that I could have watched in the garden for an hour. But then I abandoned it and found it again and rejected it and found other pleasures and came back, over and over for years. Each time I came back with new understanding. Each foray off the path taught me something I absolutely had to know in order to make progress. Nothing was ever wasted or unnecessary, even the experiences that were so painful and hard as to be almost unbearable.

Again and again, when I return to my practice after being away, whether I was away for a year or a week or only a few moments, I find an overpowering joy that nothing else can match. No matter how pleasurable the other activities seemed to be while I was doing them, when I return to my practice, I remember: nothing else comes close to this joy.

Wanting that joy again, I return to the practice. Wanting even more of it, I devote more of my life to its pursuit.

If that sounds a little like attachment, that's because it is. "Is it possible to be desireless?" Sri Satchidananda asks. "No. Actually, it is not possible. As long as the mind is there, its duty is to desire. It seems to be contradictory. But the secret is that any desire without any personal or selfish motive will never bind you." To desire more and more union with the eternal part of the Self, without attachment or aversion for particular outcomes, desiring to serve the highest part of yourself and others with compassion, is joy.

This kind of joy doesn't come to us just because we desire it. Everyone experiences moments of it in their lives, simply through grace. But to live permanently in this joy, which is the ultimate goal of yoga, requires all the practices we've described.

In this process, the pleasures and pains of the world, all the obstacles to seeing our true Self, *are transformed* from attachments and aversions into lights directing you toward the path. Pain and aversion help you to understand which way you don't want to go anymore. Yes, sometimes it takes years or decades of experiencing a pain over and over before we see what the cause is, and how we might stop it. That is simply the human condition. But the moment we first catch a glimpse of a way out of the pain and make a step in that direction, we begin the practice. Pleasure is the same: we experience the pleasures of the world and yet, after months or years or decades of that, we sigh and say to ourselves, "Somehow, I'm still not really happy. Where is my joy?" That, too, is a first glance toward the path.

Once we start to look in that direction, to practice self-study and right knowing, to understand what we have identified with or rejected, and which is the permanent source of happiness and which is the impermanent, then everything in our lives becomes a light guiding us toward joy.

Even once we see that light, though, it can seem like we're making no progress. We doubt the path. We wander away. Fortunately, the practice is always there for us, to bring us back to the quest again.

It's Personal

There was a moment in my therapy journey that almost made me give it up altogether. I had achieved a kind of stability, in that I was no longer physically hurting myself. It was possible for me to survive from one day to the next. I had enough coping skills, and enough awareness of my PTSD reactions in particular, to be able to sit through apparently intolerable emotions and come out the other side.

What I couldn't figure out was why I would want to. Why would I want to try so hard just to survive so that I could get to the next day, wake up, and try hard again just to survive? On one level, I was proud of the work I'd done and my ability to handle crushing emotional experiences without resorting to self-harm. But I was also in limbo, no longer wanting to die but with no real reason to live.

I had the same experience when I first started studying the *Sutras*. I could see that a dedicated yoga practice could lead to a life of less suffering, but as a goal, that just didn't feel worth it. I would practice when I was anxious or upset, or when I had a particular goal in mind (like becoming an instructor), then let my practice fall away again. Yoga became a coping skill and a professional aspiration, rather than a purposeful practice in itself.

It turns out that I was facing a dilemma that has divided different traditions since the very origins of yoga. For some, "the bliss of *Brahman* is countless times greater than whatever might constitute the highest level of human bliss," writes Bryant. And yet, other yoga traditions "do not speak of the experience of the liberated *purusa* [the eternal part of the self] as blissful but rather as an absence of suffering."

So is bliss the very definition of yoga, or irrelevant? Is it possible to find joy, or only the end of pain? Do we just imagine that bliss is accessible because it's a more pleasant goal to believe in?

Actually, the goal that will be most enticing for a person depends on what type of person they are. In this, as in everything else, yoga takes a pragmatic and realistic view of human nature. Not all people are the same; therefore, not all people will undertake the same practices, nor will they all be drawn to the same goal. The yoga tradition itself, Bryant notes, stands in contrast to its very close sister tradition, Sankhya. From the earliest references to these two schools, yoga is defined as an active practice: "disciplined activity, earnest striving," not a "rationalistic or intellectual" approach. Sankhya, by contrast, is almost always described as "reasoning." There's the active approach for some and the intellectual approach for others, but "the knowers of truth see that Sankhya and Yoga are one."

This distinction helped me to finally understand what I'd been reacting against in the beliefs of some of my teachers. One of my earliest teachers, for example, talked about the goal of yoga as nothingness, emptiness, the void. I know that he perceived this void as welcoming and restful and sought after it ardently, but I could not feel nothingness as a worthwhile goal. The void seemed to me not restful, but cold.

As it turns out, that teacher came from a Buddhist tradition. Like Sankhya, Buddhism has a less personal, more intellectual view of both the practice and the goal. In Buddhism, the goal is to become one with *an-atman*, "the *absence* of self." For a Buddhist, there is no such thing as an eternal Self because any notion of "self" is a form of ignorance.

Patanjali's view is the exact opposite. For him, and in his yoga tradition, the Self is "joyful, pure, and eternal," whereas everything that's painful and temporary is the "nonself." The difference can seem subtle, but in fact, according to Bryant, "the two views are thus diametrically opposed—the very goal of *yoga* and of human existence in the Yoga school is the very cause of bondage and ignorance in Buddhism."

I've tried, as much as possible, to avoid highly technical discussions of the various traditions that intertwined, and still interrelate, in Indian and South Asian history, but this difference is so important that it defines the entire purpose of what we're doing here. It's also relevant to modern yoga practitioners because so much of our current cultural interest in mindfulness and meditation draws on Buddhist concepts, whether they are acknowledged or not.

Buddhism appeals to our secular culture because it can be presented as non-theistic. Atheism is the definite belief that there is no such thing as God, whereas non-theism simply doesn't require a concept of God. Non-theistic practices are therefore accessible to a wide range of people with different beliefs. The meditation and mindfulness practices that have been packaged for Western audiences to help clear the mind or calm the nervous system are generally designed with no reference to God (or gods) or any other religious elements, and as a result, they tend to have broad appeal.

Meditation and mindfulness are powerful practices in any form, and I would never discourage anyone from using the tools available to them. Meditation in particular is one of the core practices of Patanjali's yoga. But the way most of us learn about meditation, through apps or short mindfulness exercises in a studio class, are disconnected from what Patanjali would describe as the ultimate purpose of yoga: union with the eternal Self.

Unlike Buddhism, Patanjali's yoga is, in fact, personal. The goal is not to eliminate the pesky and suffering self so that we can become part of an impersonal, eternal absence of individuality.

The goal is to remember our forgotten union with the eternal Self, a connection so blissful that everything else will seem unimportant by contrast.

Every individual practice, whether it's a physical *asana* class or a seated meditation, or breathwork, or contemplation, or any of the others, separates us just a little bit more from the bits and pieces of impermanence that we have collected around ourselves, and gets us that much closer to realizing the joy of eternal unity.

For those with a more analytical turn of mind, or a more impersonal or detached concept of the world, philosophies like Buddhism may be appealing. For those who primarily need activity and work, *karma* yoga is an option. All of the paths lead to the same place. The tradition is indeed generous.

For myself, part of the self-awareness I've developed through my own practice is that my relationship to the world is intensely personal. Despite my self-protective PTSD issues, I don't naturally step back to observe but open outward to love. Everything in the world feels alive to me, and I find my responsibility, my duty, in cherishing the personal Soul of the world. My nature is not detachment but devotion. To be in direct personal relationship with the divine is what brings me back to my practice and gives me strength to continue on my quest to realization.

A Necessary Joy

In a 1987 interview, during the recording of what would turn out to be their last album, Smiths guitarist Johnny Marr was asked his feelings about playing live. Was live performance just a necessary chore in between recording new albums?

Marr glanced up from lighting a cigarette. He seemed surprised by the question, his expressive eyebrows raising. "No," he said. "It's a necessary joy!"

That phrase has encapsulated something critical for me about the practice of yoga since the moment I first heard it. It's tattooed on my arm, in fact, where I can always see it. I've struggled to explain, to put into words, exactly what it means to me, but I know that it points to a balance in the way we pursue anything important in our lives: just because we have to do something doesn't mean it's a chore.

The ups and downs of touring with a band, the discomfort and the lack of sleep, the likelihood that something will go wrong along the way, are all unpleasant to put up with, but the moments of connection with the audience across the stage lights are the moments of joy that make the rest of it worthwhile.

Getting up early for my practice can sometimes feel pointless. Sometimes I'm just going through the motions. Even just being alive sometimes feels like too much. It's hard work. Choosing to pursue transformation and liberation in one moment does not save me from having to choose it all over again in the next moment, and then again in the next. It gets easier over time, but the effort to continue on the quest does not go away.

Doubt arises all the time. That's the nature of being human. Joy is necessary because it gives us a reason to go in a particular direction. Joy is information, telling us what matters most to us. Without joy, we might practice enough to stop suffering so much, but we would never find our way to the ultimate connection with the eternal Self. Without joy, we wouldn't know which way to turn in a world of distractions, choices, and possibilities.

Joy is necessary to take your feet from the well-trodden paths and point you toward your own practice. Without it, there would be no pull toward the more difficult, but ultimately more rewarding, goal of living as your true Self. And that's why it feels dangerous.

Transforming

Despite the fact that most don't identify as trans, drag queens have gotten caught up in the anti-transgender political panic, especially in the United States. In particular, drag story hours have been the target of a surprising amount of alarmed legislation. A drag story hour is just what it sounds like: a drag queen reading books to kids, usually in a library. These story hours have become the center of a political firestorm. But why? Why are we afraid of other people's joy?

I believe that our culture is afraid of not just drag queens, but of storytellers in general, because they speak of other ways to live. If there isn't just one possible way to be alive, one set of correct behaviors, then each person is responsible for making their own choices and their own meaning. The promise of a singular world-view is that anyone who doesn't follow that worldview will suffer for it. If I look out and see trans people, and drag queens, and others outside my worldview living in poverty and illness and homelessness, that confirms my solid ground. It keeps the tower intact. But if I look out into the world and see trans people and drag queens experiencing joy, the tower begins to crumble.

The fear is that the nature of reality itself will fundamentally change, but yoga teaches us that that is not possible. Reality is what it is. *If something can change, it isn't you.* When you fully understand that, you don't have to be afraid anymore, of someone else's joy, or your own.

In yoga, we find joy when we uncover the eternal, unchanging Self underneath all the fluctuations, all the impermanent pieces, and rediscover the union that was always within us. Experiencing even one moment of that joy will place you on the path for life. You may go away and come back, you may feel doubt and discomfort, but you will always return for the promise of that joy.

On a cultural level, joy is necessary because it is the opposite of fear. We must find our own joy and share it out loud, to show that there are many ways to live, many ways to practice, many paths all leading to the same place. Plurality is not only a personal understanding, but a cultural reality.

Ultimately, finding our joy is also a responsibility. When we find our own joy, our own connection to the eternal Self and to who we truly are, we no longer need to pass the buck of *karmic* suffering. We are no longer afraid of people who aren't on our own path. We owe it to ourselves and to each other to find our joy because true joy burns away the *kleshas*, the agonies, of living in a complicated world and leads us, instead, to compassion.

Once you have tasted that joy, you don't just want it for yourself. Just as the true Self is eternal, true Joy is infinite. It's not a hoard to keep to yourself but a limitless ocean. There is enough for everyone, and those who have tasted it want nothing more than to show everyone else how to get there, to invite them to dip their own cup, in their own way, and find bliss for themselves.

If I could start over again, be born again, have another chance at life, I would choose to be trans. That's a relatively new development for me. For a long time, I believed I would have been better off if I'd been born male. I thought, "I'm *really* male. That's how I should have been all along."

A simple, unbroken sense of myself as male would almost certainly be simpler. There would be less risk. But if I'm honest with myself, "less risk" isn't really how I live my life. Pursuing joy is a risk. Turning off the high road with only the lamp of your heart to guide you is a risk. You will encounter darkness, and you will leave behind all those who are afraid of the dark.

Just because joy is the ending, I don't want to pretend that the story is all rose petals and euphoria.

And yet—if I had to do it all over again, I would choose transness, I would choose yoga, I would choose transformation and the quest for self-realization every time. I walk in the world now, not as a man or a woman, but as a trans person, something other, and I experience love and connection and joy in ways I never believed I could.

The lessons I have learned from transness, I could not have learned any other way, and I would not give them up for any amount of ease or comfort. Likewise, the more I deepen my practice, the more I carry the eternal Self with me wherever I go. I love my silly, distractible mind and my scarred body and my wounded heart as friends so close that I will live with them until I die. But in every moment, I also feel my connection to that which will never die, the union that has always been there, waiting for me to rediscover it.

Every day, I continue to do the work of transition, which is never complete. Every day, I continue to practice clearing the brush, and opening my heart, and embracing impermanence, and letting go of attachments, and becoming more conscious of the *karmic* arrows I am releasing.

Transness has taught me that I can lay aside or change everything that I thought was my identity—my name, my gender, my roles, my appearance—and find something truer and more joyful underneath. Yoga, likewise, asks us to step back from everything we are attached to, all the fluctuations of an impermanent world, and calm the bucking bronco so that we can climb down, drop the heavy load we're carrying, and sit to watch the rising sun together.

I will see you there.

Joy is information telling us where to direct our steps on this quest. Unlike pleasure, joy is calm and steady. It is undisturbed by the comings and goings of life. I ask, "What is joy telling me about my true self? Who can I share this joy with? What light of joy is so strong that it pulls me toward it, even in darkness?"

Conclusion
Absoluteness

THE LAST OF THE FOUR SECTIONS OF THE *YOGA SUTRAS* IS called "the portion on absoluteness." It describes in detail the Nobel Prize of yoga: what we will discover when we come to live in *samadhi* not for moments at a time, but permanently. Essentially, it describes the return to the state we came from, the union from which we were separated at birth, and which we have now regained.

It's a lovely goal. I've had just enough tiny glimpses of that eternal connectedness in my practice that I come back to it again and again, seeking a little more. But I've talked a lot in this book about the end goal of our quest, and I would like to leave you, instead, with a question. I told you in the beginning that my practice was initially driven by doubt and skepticism as much as belief or faith, and that I struggled with and questioned the *Sutras* for years before coming to an understanding of them that I could commit to.

The question that I struggled with the most, and sat with the longest, was this one: *Why?*

If we were always already connected to the eternal Self in

bliss, why were we separated? If that separation is the cause of all the pain and suffering and loss that so often seem to dominate our lives, why was it allowed to happen? If connection to the eternal Self is our natural state and the ultimate form of happiness, why do we forget it, and why is it so hard to remember? Why is there this world of unhappiness and grief if we could have been connected to the eternal Self in bliss all along?

Like I said, I have wrestled with these questions for decades, and in fact the answer, or an answer, only came to me relatively recently. For me, the answer is *meaning*.

Without choice, there is no meaning, and without separation, there is no choice. Separation causes us pain. We are forced to find our own way back to connection through difficulty and against sometimes overwhelming odds. But without it, meaning is not possible.

Being separate means living as two entities at once. One is the worldly being, existing in a body and endowed with the freedom to choose. It can do anything it wants to do that it's capable of. My living being was a gift, but like any gift, it now belongs to me. I can use it to harm others or to help them, to serve the world or not, to act in whatever way I want and believe whatever I want. In this being, this incarnation, I have free will. I am also always the eternal part of myself, connected to the divine Self, yet I have to forget this in order to live in the world, to make choices, and to create the meaning of my own life.

If I have no choice but to do this or that, or believe this or that, if everything I do is predetermined, then it has no meaning. If you swear allegiance to a dictator because he will kill you otherwise, that oath is meaningless. If we were never separated from the eternal Self, we would never have the opportunity to learn, to feel, or to know for ourselves.

The eternal Self endures the pain of separation from us so that we can receive this greatest of all the gifts. That's amazing. I don't even have words for how profoundly grateful I am for this gift or how important I think it is—although that was certainly not always the case. I spent decades struggling with suicidal depression. It is not too strong to say that my practice saved me. In even my darkest moments, the dim memory of connectedness, and the promise of reunion, kept me going. In some cases, I had to endure literally one second at a time, rediscovering the reason to move forward again and again, falling into despair so deep that sometimes my entire practice was to *just not die right now.*

I hope that you never experience that feeling, but any quest worth undertaking will take you through darkness. On the other side of that darkness lies the gift of meaning, and with it, the promise of reunion.

Venturing Inward: The Practice of Freedom

The story of liberation is the most commonly repeated story in the history of literature, scripture, and myth. It's been told over and over, in many ways, through many voices, and it will continue to be told until all beings are liberated. Because our personalities and paths are different, different retellings of the story appeal to us. That's why we keep telling it in new ways.

The road to liberation is open to everyone. There are no tolls—and no express lanes. The only requirements are the desire to know your true Self and the willingness to commit to a practice.

The early yogis went into the wilderness to escape distraction and go inward to find the truth. We live, now, in an age of distractions they could not even have imagined, but the inward journey remains the same. True freedom and liberation are just like yoga, in that they are both goals and practices. Freedom is not just a state we live in or a characteristic of our situation. It's an adventure. An exploration. I had no concept, when I started practicing yoga in that strip-mall studio in South Carolina, that I would end up here.

I don't know where this practice will take me in the next 25 years, if I'm lucky enough to live that long. What I do know, without doubt, is that this is, has been, and will continue to be the most important work of my life.

My current practice, as an individual and as a teacher, focuses on the transformation of "tower moments," those times when our lives seem to be falling down around us, into moments of liberation. These moments can push us toward rigidity. They can destroy us utterly. Or they can be doorways onto the path of freedom. How does falling apart break us open? How can we transform fear, uncertainty, and chaos into expansion, authenticity, and wisdom? How do we sit with what is difficult long enough to transform it into the one lesson we need to learn?

How can we design for ourselves those practices that will clear away our brush, let our brilliant hearts shine through, and lead us to our Selves?

I have described both yoga and transness as practices of transformation rather than transformative practices. The difference matters. A transformative practice is one that happens to transform us as a result of undertaking it. Learning can transform us. Marriage certainly can. But a practice of transformation is one we undertake intentionally with the aim, the goal, of becoming something new. Learning and marriage can be practices of transformation if we choose for them to be. For that matter, yoga and transness could be neither, if we don't aim for transformation or allow ourselves to be transformed.

How you choose to achieve the goal is up to you. That is the meaning of your practice. What you choose to aim for is also up to you. That is the meaning of your life. But remember: no choice is final. Transformation is always possible. Guides and communities are available at every point along the way. And you can always choose to begin again, right now. This moment is always the moment in which you could be free.

**My choices give my life, and my practice, meaning.
In what ways can I choose to intentionally practice transformation?
Where can I make choices toward liberation for myself and for all beings? How am I making my way, one choice at a time, toward freedom?**

References and Resources

The Yoga Sutras

Here are the three translations and commentaries I cited in the book:

Edwin F. Bryant. *The Yoga Sutras of Patanjali: A New Edition, Translation, and Commentary* (New York, NY, USA: North Point Press, 2009).

Sri Swami Satchidananda. *The Yoga Sutras of Patanjali: Translation and Commentary"* (Buckingham, Virginia, USA: Integral Yoga Publications, 2020).

Swami Satyananda Saraswati. *Four Chapters on Freedom: Commentary on the Yoga Sutras of Sage Patanjali* (Munger, Bihar, India: Yoga Publications, 1976).

Two other translations and commentaries you may find helpful:

Barbara Stoller Miller. *Yoga, Discipline of Freedom: The Yoga Sutra Attributed to Patanjali* (New York, NY, USA: Bantam Books, 1998).

Nischala Joy Devi. *The Secret Power of Yoga: A Woman's Guide to the Heart and Spirit of the Yoga Sutras* (New York, NY, USA: Three Rivers Press, 2007).

The Bhakti Sutras

A.C. Bhaktivedanta Swami Prabhupada. *Narada-Bhakti-Sutra: The Secrets of Transcendental Love* (Juhu, Mumbai, India: Bhaktivedanta Book Trust, 1991).

Swami Prabhavananda. *Narada's Way of Divine Love* (Hollywood, CA: Vedanta Press, 1971).

Other Primary Sources

Eknath Easwaran, trans. *The Upanishads* (Tomales, California, USA: The Blue Mountain Center of Meditation, 2007).

Juan Mascaro, trans. *The Bhagavad Gita* (London, UK: Penguin Books, 1962).

The Origins and History of Yoga

This is in no way a comprehensive list, just a few sources that I have found useful to get you started:

Alistair Shearer. *The Story of Yoga: From Ancient India to the Modern West* (London, UK: C. Hurst & Co., 2020).

Amy Vaughn. *From the Vedas to Vinyasa: An Introduction to the History and Philosophy of Yoga* (Opening Lotus, 2016).

Deborah Adele. *The Yamas and Niyamas: Exploring Yoga's Ethical Practice* (Duluth, Minnesota, USA: On-Word Bound Books, 2009).

Jim Mallinson and Mark Singleton, eds. *Roots of Yoga* (London, UK: Penguin Books, 2017).

Swami Vivekananda. *The Four Paths of Yoga: Jnana Yoga, Raja Yoga, Karma Yoga, Bhakti Yoga* (New York, NY, USA: Discovery Publisher, 2017).

The Trans Experience and Gender Euphoria

Again, there are so many great books on this topic. These are just a few accessible collections to start your journey:

Kate Bornstein and S. Bear Bergman, eds. *Gender Outlaws: The Next Generation* (Berkeley, CA, USA: Seal Press, 2010).

Laura Kate Dale, ed. *Gender Euphoria: Stories of Joy from Trans, Nonbinary, and Intersex Writers* (London, UK: Unbound Publishing, 2022).

Micah Rajunov and Scott Duane, eds. *Nonbinary: Memoirs of Gender and Identity* (New York, NY, USA: Columbia University Press, 2019).

Acknowledgments

No book is ever the work of a single person. I have so many people to thank for their support that I am overwhelmed with the realization of how much I am supported. If I've left someone out, please know that it is not intentional. I appreciate everyone who has touched my life and led me to this place.

To all my teachers, and to the great sages and scribes who handed the yoga tradition down through centuries of practice and storytelling, my debt to you is infinite. I teach and share your tradition in part to repay what I can.

To all the queer, trans, and gender-nonconforming elders and ancestors who have made the way clearer for us, again, my debt is infinite. You have made liberation possible for so many.

To Tracy: You give therapy a good name. I truly don't know if I would be here to write this book if it weren't for our work together.

To my brother: It has truly been a joy to find our way to an adult friendship and a new kind of connection and support, despite being very different people.

To my sister: I love you, and I miss you. I hope that we can find our way back to each other.

To Mike Taigman: Your comments and feedback on the book pushed me forward at a moment when I wasn't feeling sure about anything, and your support has been instrumental.

To Chris Smith and Brody Amor: Your companionship on this transformational journey has helped to make it one of joy and light. I still strive to embody your creative spirit and your commitment to social justice.

To Rev. Dr. Angela Yarber: Without your coaching and guidance, this book that has been sitting in my heart for years would never have made it onto the page.

To my queer community in Denver, and to everyone at Rooted Heart Yoga and Wellness, thank you for offering such beautiful companionship and belonging.

Last but not least, to Islandy. Your nose fell off a long time ago, and your nubbly fabric is bare, but you've slept beside me for more than 40 years and let me hold you in the hardest and loneliest moments of my life, and to me, you are very Real.

No part of this book was written with artificial intelligence.

www.ingramcontent.com/pod-product-compliance
Lightning Source LLC
Chambersburg PA
CBHW060139150626
46550CB00015B/2043